Marcus Pankow

Component-Based Digital Movie Produc

GABLER EDITION WISSENSCHAFT

Markt- und Unternehmensentwicklung

Herausgegeben von
Professor Dr. Dres. h. c. Arnold Picot,
Professor Dr. Professor h. c. Dr. h. c. Ralf Reichwald,
Professor Dr. Egon Franck und
Professorin Dr. Kathrin Möslein

Der Wandel von Institutionen, Technologie und Wettbewerb prägt in vielfältiger Weise Entwicklungen im Spannungsfeld von Markt und Unternehmung. Die Schriftenreihe greift diese Fragen auf und stellt neue Erkenntnisse aus Theorie und Praxis sowie anwendungsorientierte Konzepte und Modelle zur Diskussion.

Marcus Pankow

Component-Based Digital Movie Production

A Reference Model of an Integrated Production System

With a foreword by Prof. Dr. Dres. h. c. Arnold Picot

GABLER EDITION WISSENSCHAFT

Bibliographic information published by the Deutsche Nationalbibliothek
The Deutsche Nationalbibliothek lists this publication in the Deutsche Nationalbibliografie;
detailed bibliographic data are available in the Internet at http://dnb.d-nb.de.

Dissertation Universität München, 2006/D19. u.d.T.: Pankow, Marcus: Component-based Digital
Movie Production – Reference Model of an Integrated Production System

1st Edition 2008

All rights reserved
© Gabler | GWV Fachverlage GmbH, Wiesbaden 2008

Editorial Office: Frauke Schindler / Sabine Schöller

Gabler is part of the specialist publishing group Springer Science+Business Media.
www.gabler.de

Cover design: Regine Zimmer, Dipl.-Designerin, Frankfurt/Main
Printed on acid-free paper
Printed in Germany

ISBN 978-3-8350-0543-3

Foreword

Digitization has an enormous impact on the media industry. While the music- and in part also the book industry have already been analyzed thoroughly under the aspect of digitization, scientific discussions are devoid of in-depth analyses regarding the possibilities and consequences of digitization in the movie and television business. Various individual aspects have indeed been discussed. However, assuming a continuous and ubiquitous digitization of production and distribution, an overview covering all aspects of entrepreneurial activities, notably in the film business, is missing. The film industry is currently still employing rather traditional criteria and has seemingly only opened itself to digitization in certain areas. There is no reason, however, why in the area of movie production the entire process could not be controlled and managed digitally. The project networks, which are the typical organization forms within the movie business, could then be set up and coordinated in a completely different way.

This view forms the background for the author's dissertation. His research questions and objectives take into account the current status of Information System Management research in this area. The author's immediate goal for his research project is to develop a specific reference model for the movie industry which could in general be utilized by a majority of film production companies; this also forms the universally applicable value of his research project. The methods have been chosen correspondingly: Information System Management - methods of reference modeling as well as case study methods have been used to allow an interchange between induction and deduction during reference modeling.

The author explains the particularities of the movie business. The various components of the value chain of movie companies are highlighted from various angles. The author discusses business strategies, different forms of organization as well as the standards for digital components in the movie production. He explains the core phrases of Strategic IS and IT Management and Strategic Enterprise Architecture Modeling important for this paper. Business modeling is introduced with reference to ARIS, and the concept of Service Oriented Architecture (SOA) is explained. The phrase Reference Modeling as well as the Unified Modeling Language (UML2) as the choice of modeling language is discussed.

An explorative case study analysis of a major movie production institution in Hollywood serves as empirical basis for the reference modeling. The author describes the current processes and structures of movie production in using Use Case Diagrams represented in UML. The reference model should consist of organizational, data, application, technical, and information architecture. The organizational architecture was established by the author through the connections between departments, actors and their respective roles. Data architecture refers to the audio-visual elements of a movie, and in respect of this the author relies primarily on MPEG-7 as descriptive language. In the application architecture one can see the connections between management and operative roles, the cinematic artifacts and the Use Cases in the sense of sub-processes. The technical architecture comprises components and services which need to be made available within the production organization. The author utilizes Service Oriented Architecture as framework for the modeling. Finally, information architecture shall highlight the dynamic aspect of the production system. The complexity of the connections to be considered for a digital illustration of the production system becomes clear.

The value of this work lies primarily in the in-depth survey and the modeling of a practice, which has not yet been analyzed in detail in scientific literature, notably the practice of movie production. The latter is particularly affected by the development in digitization. At present, it is difficult to judge whether the enterprise architecture model presented here shows sufficient dynamic and flexibility to cope with further advances in digitization which are still to be expected. In any event, this analysis enables the current changes in the movie business to be more easily examined in a systematic way. Moreover, it should greatly assist management to improve the transformation of their information and organizational structures under the influence of digitization as well as of component-based movie production. Finally, this analysis can make a significant contribution to project networks in the digital movie business to being able to receive the best possible IT-support.

Prof. Dr. Dres. h.c. Arnold Picot

Preface

New digital technologies lead to structural changes in media production, notably in the area of video production. Digitization enables the integration and support of the entire production process via a single IS platform. A practice oriented research area in the field of Information System Research is the description of an ideal configuration of computer assisted information and communication systems through reference models. This thesis aims at developing a media reference model for movie production based on digital technologies.

I developed my thesis during my work as a research assistant at the Institute for Information, Organisation and Management of the Ludwig-Maximilians-University in Munich, Germany. My sincerest thanks go to my supervisor, Prof. Dr. Dres. h.c. Arnold Picot, for giving me the opportunity and freedom to work on this dissertation. He encouraged me in my choice of subjects and supervised the development of this work favourably and with great personal and scientific interest over the past years. I am also grateful to Prof. Dr. Thomas Hess of the Institute for Information System Research and New Media of the Ludwig-Maximilians-University Munich for kindly assuming the role of second advisor and offering many helpful technical observations and comments.

In addition, I would like to thank Prof. Walt Scacchi, PhD, not only for inviting me to Donald Bren School of Information and Computer Sciences, University of California, Irvine, but also for our enlightening scientific discussions during my stay. Thank you also to Prof. Jason E. Squire of the School of Cinematic Arts, University of Southern California, for taking care of me, as well as to all the people I had the opportunity to interview in Hollywood.

Furthermore, I would like to thank my colleagues in my department at the University for their technical and personal support, notably Dr. Rahild Neuburger, Angela Sanganas, Christine Hartig, Daniela Absmayr, Quinzhao Cheng and Miguel Sanjurjo.

However, I would like to express my greatest gratitude to my family and friends, in particular my parents, my sister and her family, and my wife Katrin for continuing to encourage and support me throughout the whole period!

Marcus Pankow

Table of Contents

List of Figures

List of Tables

Abbreviations

2D	Two Dimensional
3D	Three Dimensional
3D SMax	3D Studio Max
A, M, R, D, X	Accumulate, Modify, Read, Delete, Execute
A, P, I, C	Analysis, Planning, Implementation, Control
AC	Assistant Camera Operator
ACM	Association for Computing Machinery
AD	Assistant Director
ADR	Automated Dialogue Replacement
AFM	American Film Market
AOL	America Online
ARIS	Architektur Integrierter Informationssysteme
Asst.	Assistant
BPEL	Business Process Execution Language
BPM	Business Process Management
BPR	Business Process Redesign
CA	California
CEO	Chief Executive Officer
CG	Computer Graphics
CGI	Computer Generated Imagery
CIS	Content Information Service
CLT	Chief Lighting Technician
CNN	Cable News Network
CRM	Customer Relationship Management
DB	Database
DGA	Directors Guild of America
DP	Director of Photography
DVD	Digital Versatile Disc
ERP	Enterprise Resource Planning
FFA	Filmförderungsanstalt
FR	Financial Resources

FTA	Free-to-air
FX	Effects
GoM	Grundsätze ordnungsgemäßer Modellierung
GUI	Graphical User Interface
HD	High Definition
HD Cam	High Definition Camera
HR	Human Resources
IBM	International Business Machines
ICT	Information and Communication Technology
IMDB	Internet Movie Database
IR	Intangible Resources
IS	Information System
ISO	International Organization for Standardization
IT	Information Technology
LDoc	Living Document
MAM	Media Asset Management
MCA	Music Corporation of America
MGM	Metro-Goldwyn Mayer
MM	Movie Magic
MP	Market Place
MPEG	Moving Picture Experts Group
MPEG-7	Multimedia Content Description Standard
MPEG-21	Multimedia Framework
MS	Microsoft
NAS	Network Attached Storage
NBC	National Broadcasting Company
NS	Notification
NUS	Notification Upload Service
OMG	Object Management Group
PA	Production Assistant
Post	Post-production
PR	Physical Resources

Previs	Previsualization
Prod	Production
Props	Properties
RAID	Redundant Array of Inexpensive Disks
RUP	Rational Unified Process
SAG	Screen Actors Guild of America
SAN	Storage Area Network
SCOR	Supply Chain Operations Reference Model
SD	Standard Definition
SFX	Special Effects
SOA	Service Oriented Architecture
SW	Software
TAC	Transaction Costs
TR	Technical Resources
TV	Television
UCLA	University of California at Los Angeles
UDDI	Universal Description, Discovery and Integration
UML	Unified Modeling Language
UML2	Unified Modeling Language, Version 2.0
US	United States
USC	University of Southern California
VFX	Visual Effects
VHS	Video Home System
WGA	Writers Guild of America
WS	Web Service

1 Introduction

Successful companies must continuously adapt to changing business conditions and requirements to defend their competitive advantages and to develop them for the future.[1] A modern corporate information system (IS) strategy to support the required flexibility is indispensable. One way of reducing the increasing complexity of many products and value-added processes is modularization.[2] A company concentrates on modules corresponding to its own core competencies,[3] and establishes networks with partnering companies, who fill the remaining links in the value chain.[4] Moreover, innovations of new information and communication technologies (ICT) not only accelerate the development of new products, value-added processes and value chains, but also support the management of these new organizational forms and business strategies.[5] The integration of data, functions and processes is an essential step in the development towards a fully automated enterprise – which is considered as the long-term goal of IS research.[6] I support the assumption of Scheer that the era of rigid monolithic Enterprise Resource Planning (ERP) systems has passed.[7] Service Oriented Architectures (SOA) might be a viable solution as an IS architecture approach in which both previously established and newly developed applications are encapsulated as services that can be flexibly integrated into a business process, even spanning company borders.[8]

In this thesis I will examine a modern IS strategy using the example of the motion picture industry, which, due to the current digitization in every link of its value chain, is currently in the midst of an important development process.[9] Motion pictures are complex products.[10] The prevailing organizational form of a modularized movie

---

[1] See e.g. Picot/Fiedler (2002).
[2] See e.g. Picot/Reichwald/Wiegand (2003), Picot/Dietl/Frank (2005) pp. 54, Kagermann/Österle (2006) pp. 219.
[3] See Prahalad/Hamel (1990).
[4] See Picot/Reichwald/Wiegand (2003) pp. 287.
[5] See Ibid. pp. 522, and Picot/Hass (2002).
[6] See Mertens/Bodendorf/König, et al. (2004), pp. 4.
[7] See Brocke (2003) p. 4, and Scheer (2002), p. 9.
[8] See Kagermann/Österle (2006) pp. 235.
[9] See e.g. Staden/Hundsdörfer (2003), Rüggeberg (2006).
[10] See e.g. DeFillippi/Arthur (1998).

production process is a uniquely established project network.[11] However, I will contend that there is an evident need for the production company to manage and flexibly integrate the produced digital data within the inter-organizational processes on one platform.

This introduction explains the motivation behind the thesis, narrows down the research sites and describes their epistemology. I will conclude with a summary of the other Chapters in order to explain the line of argumentation presented in this thesis.

1.1 Motivation and Research Sites

Research papers about digitization in the media industry often concentrate on individual links of the value chain, which can be divided into a production phase, a distribution phase and a reception phase.[12] Further differentiation is often made according to the form of expression of the different media products, like text, photo, audio and video files.[13] The digitization process started decades ago with small text files merely a few kilobytes in size. Today, developments in memory capacity and computing performance make the digitization of entire motion pictures financially and technically viable. This is an amazing development when one considers that a fully digitized motion picture can take up several hundred gigabytes. Scientific literature has followed this development.

In the context of printed media, Tzouvaras examined the production process of books in his thesis and developed a reference model from the perspective of the publisher.[14] In their papers on online content syndication and product platforms in the media industry, Hess et al. discuss the advantages a modularized production process – which is not only limited to the print sector – would have on the bundling and distribution phases in the value chain.[15] There are also publications on the reception phase in the print sector discussing online publications and e-books.[16]

---

[11] See e.g. Lampel/Shamsie (2003), Sydow/Windeler/Wirth (2003), Picker (2001).
[12] Schumann/Hess (2002) pp. 63 concentrates on the production, bundling and distribution phases. Zerdick/Picot/Schrape, et al. (2000) pp. 55 also integrates the recipient into the value chain. This is a relevant aspect when observing the motion picture industry.
[13] See Schumann/Hess (2002) pp. 6.
[14] See e.g. Tzouvaras (2003).
[15] See e.g. Hess/Anding (2002), Köhler/Anding/Hess (2003).
[16] See e.g. Press (2000), Dearnley/McKnight (2001), Rawolle/Hess (2000).

The impact of digitization on the music sector has been discussed extensively in recent years. Numerous papers have been published on the effects of Napster and iTunes on piracy and new modes of production and distribution.[17]

In this thesis I will concentrate on the making of video products that, considering the repetitive character of the production process, can be roughly divided into television news, fictional television series and fictional movies. Clearly the production process of highly repetitive products like television news is much more industrialized and standardized than the prototypical production process of a movie. Sydow et al. discuss television content production in Germany, concentrating primarily on television series.[18] The Pagel's thesis addresses content management systems used by TV news corporations.[19] The majority of the scientific literature in economics regarding motion pictures deals with marketing issues and is not relevant to this thesis. Motion pictures are highly speculative. It is therefore vital to make reliable box office performance predictions early on using available information such as the genre or the acting stars.[20] In recent years the distribution and reception phases of the motion picture industry have been discussed thoroughly with the designation "digital cinema".[21] A number of papers have been published on the technology behind digital cinema, the requisite worldwide standards, the influences on the parties involved, such as distributors, service providers and movie theaters, and possible working business models for the future. The Digital Cinema Initiatives, formed in 2002 by the seven major studios Disney, Fox, MGM, Paramount, Sony Pictures Entertainment, Universal and Warner Bros. Studios, released their "System Requirements and Specifications for Digital Cinema" in July 2005.[22] In view of the market power of the Hollywood majors, this specification will undoubtedly become the technological standard for digital cinema.

---

[17] See e.g. Dietl/Frank/Opitz (2005), Biren/Dutta/Wassenhove (2001), Walter/Hess (2003), and Stähler (2001).
[18] See Sydow/Windeler/Wirth (2003), Windeler/Sydow (2001).
[19] See Pagel (2003).
[20] See e.g. Neelamegham/Chintagunta (1999), Gaitanides (2001), and Frank/Opitz (2003).
[21] See e.g. Staden/Hundsdörfer (2003).
[22] Digital Cinema Initiatives (2005).

In addition to these papers, which concentrate on one specific media product, there are scientific papers dealing with the digital production, distribution and exhibition of media products in general.[23] In his thesis, for example, Hass discusses changes in media company business models brought on by developments in ICT.[24]

As previously mentioned, these developments also affect organizational forms. ICT is an enabler for virtual organizations, like the project network of a movie production. However, the motion picture industry has already been organized this way since their government regulated disintegration in the early nineteen fifties.[25]

In conclusion, to the best of my knowledge, there are no scientific studies focusing on the digital movie production process and its impacts on the IS strategies of production companies.

To fill this research gap I will examine areas of overlap between the three research domains of media management, organizational studies, and IS research.

I will argue that a flexibly integrated ICT system supporting the digital movie production offers significant potential for optimization, my goal being to develop a reference model of such a production system. In order to identify all actors and their respective activities, I will conduct an in-depth analysis of the process as a whole.[26] This will allow me to identify the requirements for an ICT system and to start modeling it.

1.2   Research Focus and Epistemology

IS research is a field of applied science combining concepts of business administration and computer science. Its goal is to develop concepts and to construct ICT systems, which support the management of information in companies.[27] In one dimension IS research takes either a descriptive and explanatory approach, or a conceptual and constructive approach. In the other dimension the subject of research

---

[23] See Schumann/Hess (1999).

[24] See e.g. Hass (2002).

[25] See Lampel/Shamsie (2003), Squire (2004).

[26] In this paper, the word "actor" is used in the generalized meaning of the word, i.e. any participant in an action or process. Where the meaning is limited to a person acting on screen or stage, I use the term "screen actor".

[27] See Wiegand/Mertens/Bodendorf, et al. (2003), pp. 9, Ferstl/Sinz (2001), pp. 1, Becker (1995), pp. 133, Scheer (1997) pp. 1, and Krcmar (2003), pp. 25.

varies with respect to domain-specific or methodological approach (see Figure 1).[28] The development of conceptual models serves the purpose of pursuing constructive goals.[29] In IS research models are a common vehicle for discussing organization and application systems.[30]

	Descriptive / Interpretive Goal	Constructive / Positivistic Goal
Domain Specific Intention	Analyzation of the Movie Production Process	Reference Modeling of a Movie Production System
Methodological Intention	Analyzation of Enterprise Architecture Models Analyzation of Reference Modeling Methods	Adaption of Established Methodologies

Figure 1: Goals of the thesis[31]

According to Stachowiak's model theory, a model is a simplified representation of an underlying reality, such as an object or a phenomenon. An idealized abstraction of the original is constructed by a modeler working with a reduced set of attributes. The modeler himself interprets the original, taking into account a given intention and a specific recipient of the model.[32]

IS models are used mainly to support implementation and decision-making processes or to represent knowledge.[33] Common modeling techniques used in software engineering are process modeling, data and function modeling or, alternatively, object modeling.[34] In combination, these techniques enable the

---

[28] See Schütte (1998), pp. 10. For a reflection on the differences in German and Anglo-American IS research approaches see e.g. Löwer (2005) pp. 8.

[29] See Brocke (2003), pp. 2.

[30] See Ibid., pp. 15, Becker/Pfeiffer (2006), pp. 3, Schwegmann (1999), pp. 7, and Schlagheck (1999), pp. 52.

[31] Based on Kugeler (2000) p. 4, Hansmann (2003) p. 7.

[32] See Stachowiak (1973), and Brocke (2003) pp. 15.

[33] See Brocke (2003) pp. 26.

[34] See Mertens/Bodendorf/König, et al. (2004) pp. 171.

extensive representation of enterprise information management in an architecture model.[35]

Reference models expand on conceptual models and have a recommending character for a variety of domains. They include domain-specific knowledge, which then serves as the development basis for further systems or models.[36] For a critical discussion on the role of reference models, their claim to universal validity and acceptance, and the question of whether these models fulfill a theory character in IS research, see Brocke and Becker.[37]

Reference modeling acquires knowledge on information management systems within enterprises using either an inductive or a deductive approach. In examining many different domains one can induce a general common practice, while the deductive approach designs reference models based upon theoretical reflections.[38]

This thesis focuses on information management in the production process of motion pictures. I will analyze the IS strategy of a production company with an orchestrator role in a project network. Thus, the thesis will pursue a domain-specific, explorative and descriptive goal, as well as having a conceptual and constructive approach resulting in a reference model. I will apply common IS research methodologies, such as engineering, as well as social science methodologies, which have been augmented to serve the needs of the thesis. Based upon theoretical considerations, I will use deduction to construct the model.

The case study research method is widely used to describe and explain phenomena in practice. It can be used as a theory building method.[39] The related action research method enables hypotheses to be tested. It requires the researcher to be closely involved in the actual development process. A cyclic approach allows the designed model to be refined and validated according to the conditions and requirements of theory and practice. As such, this research method is often used in the design of reference models.[40]

---

[35] See Krcmar (2003) pp. 28.

[36] See Tzouvaras (2003) pp 5, Brocke (2003) pp. 31.

[37] See Brocke (2003) pp. 31, Becker/Pfeiffer (2006) pp. 3, Becker/Delfmann (2004) pp. 1.

[38] See Chmielewicz (1994) pp. 101, Becker/Delfmann (2004) pp. 9, Tzouvaras (2003) pp. 5, Brocke (2003) pp. 31, Schwegmann (1999) pp. 53.

[39] See Yin (2003b) pp. 1, Yin (2003a) pp. 4, Remus (2002) pp. 7.

[40] See Remus (2002) pp. 7, Hess (1996) pp. 4.

In order to fulfill both the explanatory and the conceptual requirements of IS research I will use the case study research method in this thesis. This will give me in-depth insight into the movie production process. The quantitative examination of the hypothesis is not included in this design-engineering approach. Closer participation in practice as a researcher – as required by action research – could not be accomplished. Furthermore, due to the extensive scale of the architecture a validation of the reference model would have gone beyond the scope of a single thesis. The empirical validation of the model will therefore remain a topic for further research. In spite of the fact that the conceptual model has not yet been referenced, I will use the term "reference model" since it is my objective to develop a model which will serve as the basis for further work in this area, forming a reference for future development projects.[41]

The first research questions to be addressed are of a positive nature:

What is the prevailing organizational form used in the movie production process?

What are the essential tasks of the involved and responsible actors?

These questions aim to analyze the movie production process in detail. Exercising the case study research method, I will combine theoretical considerations, desk research and an in-depth case study of a major Hollywood movie production company. I will concentrate on the production process of internationally exploited Hollywood blockbuster productions because they are extremely versatile and their project networks normally involve every department.

The following questions address the digitization in the movie production process.

What are the impacts of digitization on the motion picture industry and the related production process?

What components are there in the motion picture industry?

What is an applicable IS strategy for a movie production company?

Motion pictures are very complex products. During the production process single modules are created and finally edited into one final movie. For years the project network of a movie production process has consisted of companies specialized on the delivery of such components. Nowadays, digitization in every step of the

---

[41] Remus (2002) pp. 7

production process supports the modularization even more effectively. An appropriate IS strategy concept must be found that takes into consideration all the requirements of the movie production process and especially the implications of digitization for data management.

This work forms the basis for the constructive part of this research, answering the following normative questions:

How should the IS strategy of a production company be oriented so as to best support the project network of a movie production process?

How should the IS strategy be oriented so as to support the production of digital component-based contents?

How should a production system be structured so as to integrate the inter-organizational processes on one platform?

These three questions underline the significance the organizational form "project network" has for a production company. The producer acts as an orchestrator in the network, managing inter-organizational collaboration during the production process. Digitization has enormous optimization potential that can be utilized if the producer provides an integrated platform. This will be shown in the following Chapters, concluding with a proposed enterprise architecture model.

This model is constructed from the viewpoint of a major Hollywood production company. In my analysis I concentrate on big blockbuster productions to cover every important aspect of the movie production process. But the model is not limited to this scenario. In the development process a reference model serves as a basis, which is then adapted to meet the actual requirements.

I argue that if a complex and prototypical movie production process benefits from an integrated production system, less complex movie productions, as well as productions with a higher degree of industrialization that are produced on a regular basis, such as TV films, series or news broadcasts, would also benefit from such a production system.[42]

Therefore, this thesis pertains not only to the IS departments of Hollywood majors but also to their international competitors, like German media production companies that might find competitive advantages in exploiting this essential milestone on the way to a fully digitized motion picture value chain. The findings of this thesis are of relevance to all movie production companies, and as result the presented model has the potential to become the prevalent reference model for the industry.

1.3 Chapter Overview

My research methodology and line of argumentation are set out in Figure 2 and the following Chapter overview.

In Chapter One I defined the goal of this thesis, narrowed down the scope of research and explained the chosen methodology. The main goal of this thesis is to analyze the motion picture production process in detail with a focus on the underlying IS strategy. As a result I will present a reference model of an integrated production system that enables production companies to manage every individual step of a digital movie production. There are few publications on IS strategy in the motion picture industry. It is, therefore, necessary to gather theoretical information on IS strategy and combine it with an empirical analysis of the movie production process. On this basis I will then deduce a reference model of the production system.

Chapter Two will start with a description of the motion picture industry as a part of the media industry, elaborating the specifics of the value chain and the movie as a product. In discussing different business strategies I will conclude that the prevailing form of organization in a movie production process is the project network. The progressive digitization of products and processes allows for new ways of coordination and collaboration in such a network on the one hand, and provides a more efficient way of managing the produced content elements on the other. This Chapter forms the theoretical basis for the domain "motion picture industry". The

---

[42] On content management systems for TV stations see the thesis of Pagel (2003), the Dalet Plus NewsSuite by Dalet (2006) and the Digital Media Framework by IBM (2006).

project network, as an organizational form, requires inter-organizational collaborative business processes. The modularization and digitization of the production process make possible the high degree of content reusability integrated media companies are striving for. All these considerations must be taken into account by the IS strategy.

In Chapter Three I will specify IS management tasks and how to create an information management strategy. After that I will describe the elements of an integrated enterprise model and show ways of designing the same. I will show that the Service Oriented Architecture is the model of choice for a production system. As my goal is the creation of a reference model, I will also explain the concept of reference modeling procedures.

I have chosen the case study research method to gain insight into the movie production process. In Chapter Four I analyze the responses from twelve narrative expert interviews held with studio executives of a major Hollywood movie production company in 2004. To structure the production process and the interviews, I adapted the rational unified process, a software engineering process model, for use in the motion picture industry. The results of the explorative case study are specified in use case models of the movie production process for each phase of the production.

Results from the case study comprise the fundamental data upon which the following reference modeling process is based. This data is subsequently used to develop an integrated enterprise architecture model in Chapter Five. Together with the intermediate results from the theoretical Chapters, the use cases deliver the requirements to be fulfilled in the reference model. I will start modeling the organizational architecture by analyzing the involved departments and the actors in the production network. I will then construct a data architecture model referencing the MPEG-7 standard for the description of digital movie elements. In the application architecture I will describe and cluster the use cases from the case study into functional components. In the technical architecture model I will construct functional components, such as web services that are accessed by a central business process management server. Finally, I will deal with the information architecture by modeling the collaborative business processes throughout the different phases of the production process. The resulting reference model will comprise the models generated in these five steps.

The final Chapter summarizes the results of this thesis and discusses the applicability and limitations of the model. I will attempt to give an overview of the implications of applying such integrated production systems and conclude with an outlook on further practical and research aspects.

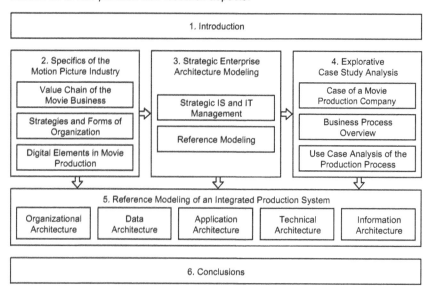

Figure 2: Structure of the Thesis

2 Specifics of the Motion Picture Industry

In this Chapter I will give an outline of the motion picture industry with the movie as its product. I will describe the value chain of media products in general and of the product "movie" in particular. I will then focus on the production process of a movie and describe the project network as the prevailing organizational form. The Chapter will end with an exposition of the technical transformations in the motion picture industry today, mainly the ongoing digitization. I will also describe the efforts of the Moving Picture Experts Group (MPEG) to create notational standards like MPEG-7 and MPEG-21 for the description of digital content elements. This Chapter will clarify the strategic challenges in the motion picture industry which have direct implications on the strategic IS management.

2.1 Value Chain and Profit Window Chain of the Movie Business

To examine the value chain in the motion picture industry I first describe the concept of value chains in general and their significance for strategic management and strategic information systems.

Porter's concept model of the value chain gives a representation of the value-creating processes of an enterprise.[43] Strategic management uses this customer-centric, intra-organizational and process-based model to analyze the profit margin as the difference of the total customer value and the costs for the value-creating activities.[44] To effectively reveal the value drivers and their costs, the value chain is divided into primary and supporting activities, which are examined individually (see Figure 3).

---

[43] See Porter (2000).
[44] See Zerdick/Picot/Schrape, et al. (2000) pp. 31.

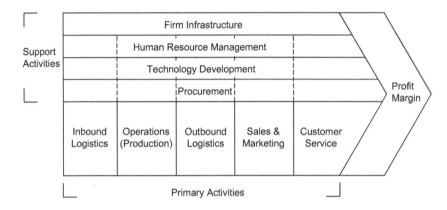

Figure 3: Porter's Value Chain[45]

The value chain of an enterprise is interconnected with the preceding and subsequent value chains of suppliers and customers, expanding to a value system covering every raw material and further input factor needed to produce a good of given value for the customer.[46] Supply chain management concepts and models ensure that no value is lost in the interconnections between the individual value chains in the value system. The Supply Chain Operation Reference (SCOR) framework, consisting of different abstraction levels and the five phases plan, source, make, deliver and return, is a widely accepted reference model for the execution of inter-organizational processes.[47] However, before a complex inter-organizational supply chain model like the SCOR model can be applied to media productions, their internal processes, technical specifications and creative character should be optimized and supported by information technology .

A business process is a bundle of activities, in which a number of input factors are transformed into an output that is of value for the customer. Business Process Reengineering (BPR), developed in the early 90s, is a concept in which a company focuses on its core competencies, the critical customer centric business processes are fundamentally redesigned and information technology is excessively applied to

---

[45] Based on Porter (2000) p. 66.
[46] See Zerdick/Picot/Schrape, et al. (2000) pp. 31.
[47] See Supply Chain Council (2005a), Supply Chain Council (2005b), Bolstorff (2001)

support these processes.[48] The subsequent and expanding Business Process Management (BPM) concept enables an organization to implement a continuous process improvement culture, which optimizes quality, duration and costs of the business processes.[49] To achieve these goals, BPM is focused on process integration and collaboration. It is not limited to the internal processes, but rather integrates them with the management of inter-organizational business processes and supply chains and with Customer Relationship Management (CRM).[50]

After this brief introduction of value chain management and process management, the following paragraph concentrates on the specifics of the media industry and value chain in the motion picture industry, which then forms the basis on which I will develop my reference model framework.

The motion picture industry can be seen as a section of the media industry. Media companies produce, bundle and distribute information or entertainment content for a mass market.[51] To store, transport and present the information goods to the recipients,[52] media products are tied to media platforms that can be distinguished as print and storage media as well as broadcast and data networks.[53] Furthermore, media companies can be categorized by the different forms of media used to transport their product content, like books, newspapers, journals, movies, television, radio, music, video games, and the internet.[54] Media products generate revenues in two different markets. The information or entertainment content per se represents the value a recipient is willing to pay for, while the presentation of the information through a mass medium that commands the attention of an audience, which can, in turn, be sold on the advertising market.[55] Media products are experience products and, in contrast to other consumer goods, have a non-rival character: they are intangible assets that do not lose value when they are consumed repeatedly by one or by many

---

[48] See Hammer/Champy (1994)

[49] See also Hammer (1997) pp. 33, Gaitanides/Scholz/Vrohlings (1994) pp. 16.

[50] See Jost/Scheer (2002) pp. 33.

[51] See Schumann/Hess (2002) pp. 9, Schulze (2005) pp. 24, and Wirtz (2003) pp. 9. Compare also Altmeppen (2003) pp. 19, and Sjurts (2002) pp. 5.

[52] For an introduction to information goods see Hass (2002) pp. 38.

[53] See Schumann/Hess (2002) pp. 6, Tzouvaras (2003) pp. 15, Schulze (2005) pp. 24, Sjurts (2002) pp. 8, and Hass (2002) pp 77.

[54] See Wirtz (2003) pp. 21, Schumann/Hess (2002) pp. 6.

[55] See Schumann/Hess (2002) pp. 22, Sjurts (2002) pp. 8, Zerdick/Picot/Schrape, et al. (2000) pp. 38.

recipients.[56] Industrialization of production processes in the media industry is not trivial since the value of the prototypic production often relies on creative artists and talents, which makes it extremely difficult to predict the potential output value of the assets in advance.[57] However, because of this necessity, most marketing-related scientific literature about the movie industry discusses prediction models.[58]

The general value chain of a media production can be divided into the phases: creation, selection, configuration, and distribution. Figure 4 describes the value chain of a media product which is sold on two markets, the recipient-market as well as on the advertising-market. Tzouvaras explains the single phases in detail.[59]

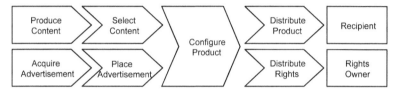

Figure 4: Value chain of media enterprises[60]

Bearing the specifics of a movie production in mind, it seems appropriate to alter the value chain model by naming the advertising phases: "invest in product" and "sell product". From the illustration of the value chain one can build up the X-model for media productions as a reference model framework.[61] The X-model can be seen in Figure 5. During my modeling process I will concentrate on the production process, leaving out the advertising market and the distribution of the content.

---

[56] See Zerdick/Picot/Schrape, et al. (2000) pp. 31 and pp. 38, Tzouvaras (2003) pp. 15.

[57] See Zerdick/Picot/Schrape, et al. (2000) pp. 38.

[58] See e.g. Neelamegham/Chintagunta (1999), Ainslie/Drèze/Zufryden (2002), Simonoff/Sparrow (2000), Moe/Fader (2002), Eliashberg/Swami/Weinberg, et al. (2003), Reinstein/Snyder (2000), Sharda/Delen (2002), and Elberse/Eliashberg (2002).

[59] See Tzouvaras (2003) pp. 43

[60] Based on Ibid. p. 43

[61] See Schumann/Hess (2002) pp. 116

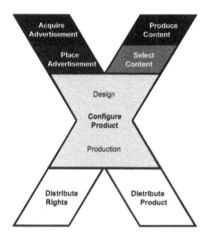

Figure 5: X-Model of media enterprises[62]

In Figure 6 Zerdick et al. give a brief overview of the film production value chain, the responsible actors for the different phases and some examples of activities for each of the phases.[63] Unclear in this figure is the representation of the returning revenues. Zerdick et al. want to point out that the returning revenues finance the preceding production steps. They also mention that in this figure the important financing steps, as well as the end customer, the moviegoer, are not explicitly included.

However the investment must be done in the pre-production phase, at which point it is practically impossible to predict the potential value of the produced assets. Therefore, in a value chain model it is appropriate to integrate the financing, which is done by investors and exploiters, predicting the potential market value of the asset defined by the demand of the end costumer.[64]

---

[62] Based on Tzouvaras (2003) pp. 45.
[63] See Zerdick/Picot/Schrape, et al. (2000) pp. 55.
[64] See also Hass (2002) who includes the recipient in his models.

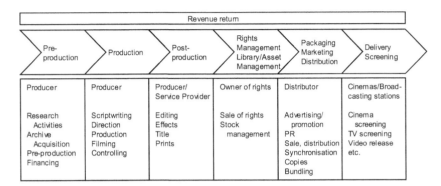

Figure 6: Value chain for film production[65]

Both representations, the general media value chain and the value chain for film production, give a first and rough overview, but are both insufficient for my approach to extensively discuss the motion picture production process. Hence, I create my own reference model framework later on. For further explanations on reference models and reference model frameworks see 3.2.

The motion picture industry uses a series of different exploitation windows to sell their rights.[66] A produced movie is sold to an audience via independent cinema chains. In the US this step sells only the product to the customer, whereas in Europe in addition a buoyant and expensive movie advertising market exists and the audience has to watch roughly 20-40 minutes of advertisements before viewing the movie. But also in the US, the audience and their attention in cinemas are used, if only indirectly. The higher the success of a movie at the cinema, the higher the price for the rights sold through further exploitation windows. The next exploitation steps are home entertainment, video-on-demand and pay-TV, where the audience pays for the delivery of the desired information goods. The window that follows is free-to-air (FTA), where the rights are sold at prices dependent on the consumer attention a movie generates.

Not only the advertising market uses the attention a movie and its content generate. The integrated Hollywood studios use their diverse channels to cross-sell related

---

[65] Based on Zerdick/Picot/Schrape, et al. (2000) p. 56.

[66] See Zerdick/Picot/Schrape, et al. (2001).

products and thus broaden their potential revenue streams. In the last few years, as the concentration of the big media conglomerates progressed and new technologies enabled new business models, many papers were written regarding the multiple use of content. But this strategy is nearly as old as the American studio system as can be seen in Figure 7, a diagram from the year 1957 in which Disney shows how to generate and exploit assets throughout the many departments of the enterprise.

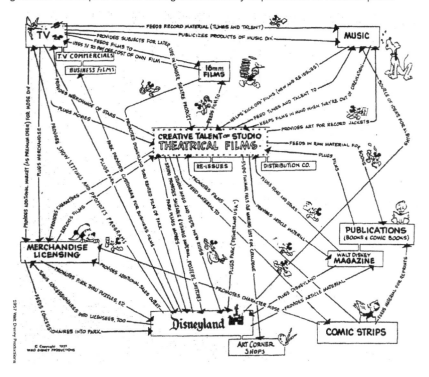

Figure 7: Disney's asset model from 1957[67]

---

[67] Published in the New York Times, kindly provided by Prof. Walt Scacchi, Donald Bren School of Information and Computer Sciences, University of California, Irvine.

2.2   Business Strategies and Forms of Organization

In finding an appropriate IS strategy one has to consider the company's strategy. As mentioned above two extraordinary transformations can be observed in the movie industry. One is the ongoing digitization. Modern ICT systems influence production, distribution and consumption of the product, as well as the management and the organization of the media enterprises.[68] The second transformation is the ongoing integration process of the biggest entertainment companies, as can be seen in the merger of NBC and Universal or AOL Time Warner, and Viacom.[69] Information systems not only make it easier to manage these big companies; they also support different organizational strategies.[70]

Basically there are three major strategies for the ideal organizational implementation of the value chain in the movie business: the strategy of core competencies, the integration strategy and the network strategy.[71] Following the strategy of core competencies, the company has the option of concentrating on one particular step of the value chain.[72] By focusing their abilities they can claim an extraordinary position in the competition. Companies that are in a restructuring process often sell parts of their business units if they do not focus on their core competence, as happened with Babelsberg Filmstudios in Berlin, sold by NBC Universal.[73] A second implementation example for this strategy can be seen in the fact that the major Hollywood movie production company does not have its own animation studio. A small company such as Dreamworks, which is specialized in the field of animation, is in a position to work more efficiently. However, for the global distribution of a motion picture another strategic management option is necessary: the integration strategy.[74]

Vertical integration in the motion picture industry means the integration of preceding or subsequent links in the value chain. The goal is to secure the supply and trade channels. The integration of production steps is a management opportunity, as long as the price for a specific step is higher on the market or the transaction is very

---

[68] See Shapiro/Varian (2000)
[69] See McClintock/Demspey (2004).
[70] See Zerdick/Picot/Schrape, et al. (2005) pp. 5.
[71] For the following, see also Wirtz (2003) pp. 70.
[72] See Prahalad/Hamel (1990).
[73] See Whiteman (2004).
[74] See Wirtz (1999).

uncertain and complex.[75] These arguments, and of course the possibility to force one's own market power onto other steps in the value chain, is one reason for the merger of NBC and Universal.

Horizontal integration is expanding the activities in one step of the value chain. Very often it is used to enter foreign markets or a new market segment. The advantages are economies of scale and scope. A good example of horizontal integration can be found in the television stations of NBC Universal, which are specialized on certain target groups in order to increase advertising revenue.

Following the network strategy, companies are organized into cooperative groups working together on the value-added process. This consolidation can be horizontal and vertical.[76] The network-forming companies stay legally independent and are only united by a common objective target.[77] The big advantage is the coexistent use of the integration strategy and the strategy of core competencies. The formation of business webs is often found in capital-intensive industries with high innovation pressure and high risk, like the co-production of motion pictures.[78] Sydow has shown that the prevailing organizational form in movie production is the project network. The project network is a special form of a business web with the characteristic that the network is formed for just one specific project.[79] The actors involved in such a project network are kept in a so-called "pool" after decomposition of the network. From there they might be selected again for participation in a future job.[80]

The make or buy strategy is closely interdependent on the three strategies described above. The make or buy strategy refers to a major studio's optimal depth of involvement in the product development process.[81] There are effectively two extremes with many hybrid forms in between. A major production company can make the product and distribute it itself or can buy the rights of an externally produced film to distribute it. Advantages and disadvantages can be listed for both management strategies. If they only buy the rights, one speaks of production outsourcing.

---

[75] See Heinrich (1999) pp. 38 and for detailed information about transaction theory see Picot/Dietl/Frank (2005) pp. 46.
[76] See also Albarran (1997)
[77] See Backhaus/Piltz (1990)
[78] On business webs see also Steiner (2005)
[79] See Sydow/Windeler (2002) and Sydow/Windeler/Wirth (2003)
[80] See Picker (2001)
[81] See Wirtz (2003) pp. 77

It is well known that the production process is very risky. To outsource production might be an advantage. A production can run out of money or out of time, and the costs the company incurs are sunk-costs, meaning that the money for the production has to be paid even though the studio does not know in advance whether anyone will buy the product. If the product cannot be sold all the costs are sunk. By outsourcing the production a studio can take the decision on whether to buy a product after it has screened the result.

New technologies such as digitization and internet-technologies, as well as ongoing globalization must also be taken into account. One can now buy products or just modules from firms specialized in digital effects, for example. A production company can reduce their transaction costs by finding network partners through internet services. And finally, digital production elements can be created in countries where production costs are lower.

On the other hand though, these new technologies give studios the option of producing at lower cost and to pursue the make strategy. A very important advantage of this strategy is that the studio stays in control of the product quality and has power over the company's profile by producing in-house. There is no general solution to this management problem – each case has to be decided individually. A studio has to consider both strategy opportunities.

2.3 Digital Elements and Components in Movie Production

Modularization in the media industry, especially in movie production, refers to the option of producing content in individual modules or components. The content has to be separated from its communication medium, which in analog productions is the celluloid film. Furthermore the content has to be separated from its layout. By doing so, one gets single modules which are stored in content management systems – so called media neutral databases – and can easily be used to create new combinations of content. The options for creating new products out of certain modules are limited by the semantics. The limitations are larger in very complex modules.

An illustrative and functioning example of this technique is the archive of a news corporation like CNN. Their news suite, the Media Production Suite by IBM, whose current version is called Digital Media Center, supports the editorial process of a news channel by very efficiently extracting modules like pictures, movie scenes and music on a specific topic. The basic problem of such a system is the retrieval of stored content. It is therefore crucial that the created content is described very carefully. The more ways there are to shoot a given scene, the more alternatives there are in describing the scene.

The new standards MPEG-7 and MPEG-21 will help solve this problem in the future.[82] MPEG, the Moving Pictures Experts Group, is a working group of ISO, the International Standards Organization. MPEG-7, formally named "Multimedia Content Description Interface", is a standard for describing multimedia content data. MPEG-21 is a "Multimedia Framework" in which content is separated into digital elements, giving information on how a user can interact with items and how they are interconnected. MPEG-21 uses the description language MPEG-7.

Like news corporations, a movie production studio can also benefit from MPEG-7. Modern film production uses many different layers in each frame. Examples are StarWars 3, Lord of the Rings or purely digital movies like Final Fantasy. Each layer can be an object like a digital or a human character, or a background, which can be painted, digitally created or shot with a camera. The post-production process can get extremely expensive, as most of the layers are created in post-production and the amount of elements that have to be managed keeps increasing. So, these new techniques would first be used in production.

Furthermore some projects are designed as feature films, DVD releases, computer games or TV-series. An asset management system supporting the MPEG-7 description language makes it easier for different departments to find and use the produced modules to build up their specific products.

2.4 Summary

In this Chapter I have given an overview of the movie business as one part of the entertainment industry. I have explained the value chain and the production processes of a motion picture. Furthermore, I have described the business strategies of production companies, focused on the project network as the prevailing form of organization and have subsequently described the changing requirements and technological achievements through ongoing digitization in every step of the value chain. These new technologies enforce the tendency for transforming studios into flexible, knowledge-intensive organizations that are more flat than hierarchical.

---

[82] See Martinez (2004)

These developments are certain to affect the information technology of a production company. In the following Chapter I will explain the concept of strategic enterprise architecture and how it supports the management of the most valuable good of a production company – the created digital content.

3 Strategic Enterprise Architecture Modeling

In this Chapter I will define the terms strategic IS management and enterprise architecture. My objective in this thesis is to create a reference model of an integrated production system. To this end I will explain reference models in general, the modeling process and the notation I chose for my concept. At the end of this Chapter I will develop a meta-model which both the empirical case study analysis in Chapter 4, as well as the reference model in Chapter 5 are based on.

3.1 Strategic IS and IT Management

Information systems (IS) and information technology (IT) management are responsible for managing the lifecycle of information that is used within and produced by the enterprise.[83] Mertens et al. name three prerequisites for reaching this goal: defining an information systems strategy, defining the information systems architecture and finally choosing the necessary IT projects for implementation.

In order to find an IT and IS strategy one has to examine the actual evolution stage of the company's IT and the desired roadmap. Porter describes five stages, automation of transaction, functional enhancement of activities, cross-activity integration, integration of the entire value chain, and the optimization of various activities in the value chain in real time.[84] Mertens emphasizes the fifth stage by seeing the enterprise within an integrated network of partnering companies in which automated supply chains are managed flexibly and collaboratively across enterprise boundaries. Therefore, an IS and IT management strategy has to correspond to the enterprise's overall strategy, including their suppliers, alliance partners, distributors and customers, viewed as a single business system.[85]

A well-known reference model for developing an integrated enterprise architecture model is the ARIS house of business engineering as shown in Figure 8. ARIS (Architecture of Integrated Information Systems) offers a methodology for designing an enterprise model by integrating different static and dynamic views of the enterprise. The organization, data, function and output view build the static structure of the system and the control view connects the static components via the business processes. The model also integrates the enterprise strategy as well as the existing

---

[83] See Mertens/Bodendorf/König, et al. (2004) pp. 187
[84] See Porter (2001) p. 74
[85] See also Chan (2005) pp. 148

and upcoming IT infrastructure. An architecture model has a certain level of abstraction. The ARIS house of business engineering focuses on the analysis and requirements definition level.[86] There are numerous similar approaches to enterprise modeling, but most of them have four basic views in common: organization, data, function and control.[87]

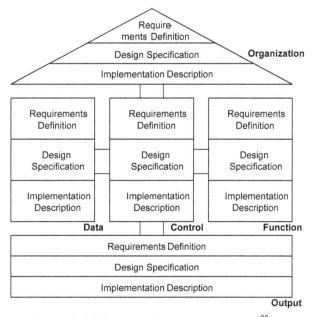

Figure 8: ARIS house of business engineering[88]

For each view, specialized modeling techniques have been established. As one specific example, the Unified Modeling Language currently standardized by the Object Management Group (OMG) in version 2.0 (UML2) offers an integrated toolset of notations and diagrams to support an enterprise-modeling project. UML2 uses different abstraction levels to enable high level business process modeling as well as object-oriented modeling with classes, attributes and operations that are close to implementation level and can be translated into source code. To model an

---

[86] For further information on ARIS see e.g. Scheer (2002)
[87] See also Picot/Reichwald/Wiegand (2003) pp. 221
[88] Based on Scheer (2002) p. 4, Schütte (1998) p. 90.

organizational architecture by extracting information from the organization view, UML2 offers static structure diagrams like class or component diagrams.

As mentioned above, the goal of a modern IT and IS strategy is to reach the fifth development stage. It is defined by a high integration rate of data, functions and business processes across firm boundaries. To enable collaborative business processes, the IT and IS architecture has to fulfill certain requirements. The evolution of information system development concepts has moved from a functional approach to an object-oriented approach. Objects support easier reusability by encapsulating the inner state and behavior of the object and offering well defined interfaces. Objects can be combined intelligently to a single component, with qualities similar to an object, albeit on a higher abstraction level.[89] To enable integrated collaborative business processes, functional components have to be accessed via the internet protocol. These components are therefore encapsulated as web services, offering well defined interfaces to access their service over the internet. The resulting enterprise architecture model is the Service Oriented Architecture (SOA) as shown in Figure 9.[90]

SOA translates the different views of the enterprise into layers. Each layer offers a service via specified interfaces to its upper layer. Service execution is transparent to a calling layer. The base layer is the data layer in which the enterprise's data is stored within databases. The databases are accessed by functional components representing the component layer. The components are encapsulated into web services; therefore the core web services layer offers the interfaces access to the functional components. On top of the web service layer is the composition and choreography layer. The composition layer controls automatic access to the web services, whereas the choreography layer represents the business processes. The graphical user interfaces can be found on top of the choreography layer.

---

[89] See Oestereich (2005) pp. 17
[90] For this and for the following see Keen/Adinolfi/Hemmings, et al. (2005)

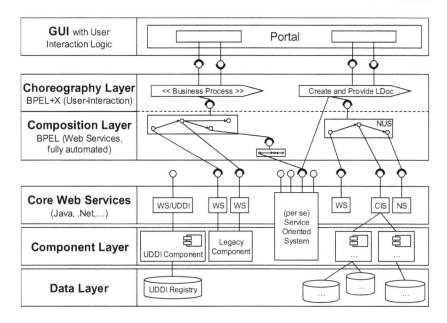

Figure 9: Service Oriented Architecture[91]

3.2 Reference Modeling

A reference model is a generalized model of elements in a system constructed using a predefined language. This generalized model, with its recommending character, then serves as a foundation for specialized models or implementations. Reference models can be modeled inductively, by analyzing a large number of different enterprise-specific models and by combining them into one generalized model. The other approach is to construct the model deductively based upon theoretical considerations. The model's character - normative or positive - can then be used to discriminate between the resulting reference models.[92] In building the reference model, one can choose between concentrating on structure-based or on behavior-based models. The abstraction levels of the system description and of the generic types also have to be defined in advance: is it a business concept, an IT system concept or possibly already an implementation concept? Are the generic types

---

[91] Based on Abeck (2005).
[92] See Tzouvaras (2003), pp 5 and Schütte (1998), pp 69.

implemented in a company-specific manner or are they generalized – or is there only a meta-level syntax definition?[93]

The reference model level of quality should be secured by following strict principles during the modeling process.[94] Required principles are correctness, relevance and economic efficiency. The models must be syntactically and semantically correct. Only relevant information should be modeled. The complexity of the model is restricted by economical constraints. Supplementary principles are clarity, comparability, and systematic structure.

The reference modeling process can be divided into four phases. First the desired reference model has to be classified. In this phase the discriminators described earlier are selected in such a way that the model can best address a given problem. Next, a framework that structures the model elements on a high meta-level is chosen. In the third phase the reference model is built. Following the framework, structure elements are modeled observing modeling principles. The result is a functional reference model. To test the model and to find possible errors, the reference process is verified in a practical environment in phase four.[95]

For my reference model, I chose the UML2 modeling notation. I model use case diagrams during the explorative case study analysis at the major Hollywood movie production company to gain insight into the production process and the involved actors. Then I use static class and component diagrams to model the organizational structure of the production network and the structure of the technical artifacts. Finally I model business processes using activity diagrams. For detailed information on UML2 and their modeling components, please refer to the literature.[96]

My reference model can be classified as a normative model. To gain an initial positive overview of the general process, I collected detailed empirical information about the production process at one enterprise and combined it with general information that was gathered from literature review. The desired reference model, by contrast, is not meant to show the actual state. Deducing from literature review of the state-of-the-art architecture models, I will construct a normative reference model. A

---

[93] See Schütte (1998), pp 64
[94] For the following see Ibid. pp. 119 and Tzouvaras (2003) pp. 10
[95] See Tzouvaras (2003) pp. 24
[96] For example see Oestereich (2005)

normative reference model cannot be verified easily as demanded in phase four of the reference modeling process.

As mentioned above, the reference model will include structure- as well as behavior-based views. The abstraction level will be an IT system concept, defining generic types.

I will adopt the Rational Unified Process (RUP) as a framework for my reference modeling process.

4 Explorative Case Study Analysis

In order to model an IT system supporting the digital movie production process, it is necessary to gather detailed information about the process, the activities, the actors and the created artifacts in each step. The basic research questions aim at a descriptive goal: "how is the movie production process organized?" and "how does the ongoing digitization influence the process?"

In this study I will concentrate on the first question, building up a detailed requirements analysis. To obtain the necessary information I will use a qualitative empirical study in conducting narrative expert interviews with twelve executives of a major Hollywood movie production company.

The case study research method is the one most suitable for my survey. Yin defines case studies as "an empirical inquiry that investigates a contemporary phenomenon within its real-life context, especially when the boundaries between phenomenon and context are not clearly evident."[97] A case study is the preferred method when the predominant research questions are "how" and "why".[98]

The case study method allows the combination of different forms of data collection such as archives, interviews, questionnaires and observations. The collected data can be qualitative, quantitative or even both.[99] Case studies can have different aims. Explorative case studies explore a phenomenon in practice and lead to new theories, while in descriptive case studies a phenomenon is described; the explanatory case study tries to explain a phenomenon.[100]

For my research purpose, the analysis of the movie production process, I chose an in-depth, descriptive case study. I will examine the movie production process based on twelve narrative expert interviews with executives of major Hollywood movie production company, combined with published company data and personal observations. Furthermore, a general literature review about the movie production process is included.

---

[97] Yin (2003b), p. 13
[98] Ibid., p. 1
[99] Eisenhard (1989), p. 534
[100] Yin (2003b), p. 5

The interviews took place in summer 2004 at a major Hollywood movie production company. Following the information policy of the company, the quoted interview partners do not want to be called by name. The company data is freely available on the internet. My personal observations were made during my collaboration on the set of the 15-minute short movie production "Entity: Nine" at the School of Cinema-Television at the University of Southern California.[101] Further observations could be made during visits to the major Hollywood movie production company. In the summer of 2004 I joined the Movie Business Seminar of Prof. Jason E. Squire at the School of Cinema-Television, to learn about the Hollywood entertainment industry, and in particular the movie production process. His book is an important source of my a-priori understanding of the process.[102] It was through this course that I was also able to get in contact to the executives of the major Hollywood movie production company and to ask my specific questions.

The following is a listing of the interviews conducted at a Hollywood studio location:

- Interviewee_1, Production Services, interview held on July 1, 2004

- Interviewee_2, Creative Executive, Motion Picture Production, interview held on July 1, 2004

- Interviewee_3, President of Physical Production, interview held on July 8, 2004

- Interviewee_4, Senior Vice President Physical Production, interview held on July 8, 2004

- Interviewee_5, Business Affairs, interview held on July 8, 2004

- Interviewee_6, President of Marketing, interview held on July 15, 2004

- Interviewee_7, Producer and Editor, interview held on July 15, 2004

- Interviewee_8, Executive Vice President of General Sales, interview held on July 22, 2004

- Interviewee_9, Executive Vice President of General Sales, interview held on July 22, 2004

---

[101] See IMDB (2006), Kean (2004).
[102] Squire (2004) gives an overview of the movie business.

- Interviewee_10, President Worldwide Home Entertainment, interview held on July 22, 2004

- Interviewee_11, Vice President Interactive, interview held on July 29, 2004

- Interviewee_12, Global Marketing and Media Consultant, interview held on July 30, 2004 at USC

4.1 The Case of a Major Hollywood Movie Production Company

The following Chapter summarizes the results of the in-depth case study of the major Hollywood movie production company and the movie production process.

After a short overview of the major Hollywood movie production company I will describe the movie production process phase by phase, from development to the end of post-production. My goal is to analyze and to structure the different activities in each phase and to assign them to different core or supporting processes. I will identify the actors involved and their responsibilities and describe the milestone at the end of each phase.

The analysis follows the structure:

- Description of the phase and its sub-phases

- Description of the identified processes within the phase

- Description of the activities in the different processes

- Description of the actors involved in these activities

- Description of possible iterations of the phases

- Description of the milestone at the end of the phase

The use case diagrams designed with the Unified Modeling Language are the basis to model the respective business processes. The models for the complicated production processes are already divided into the different core and supporting processes. Most of the information compiled in the use case diagrams will not be elaborated on further in the text.

4.2 Overview of a Major Hollywood Movie Production Company

The seven major studios in Hollywood, 20th Century Fox, Columbia, Disney, MGM/United Artists, Paramount, Universal and Warner Brothers control the worldwide market of motion pictures.

They have in common the integration of studio facilities (except for MGM, which never owned its own sound stages), production companies and a worldwide network of distribution companies.[103] Nowadays, the studios are part of global media and entertainment conglomerates that can easily exploit movie rights alongside theater distribution via channels such as TV, video, music, merchandising or video games. Fox is a division of News Corporation, Columbia and MGM are divisions of Sony, Paramount is a division of Viacom, Universal is a division of General Electric and Warner Brothers is a division of Time Warner. To date, only Disney has remained independent.[104]

The focus of this analysis is the movie production process in a major studio. The value of the major studios are the film libraries they have built up over decades and their ability to exploit the corresponding rights via diverse channels.

The major Hollywood movie production company produces and distributes theatrical and non-theatrical motion pictures. It creates a diverse mix of high-quality content, which is then exploited via television, home video, the recreation business, consumer products and other ancillary businesses. Its focus is the creation of franchises with long-term branding opportunities across all their businesses.

The following diagram illustrates the task division between the production and distribution of a major Hollywood movie production company (see Figure 10).

---

[103] Keil/Iljine (2000), p. 110
[104] Squire (2004), p. 9

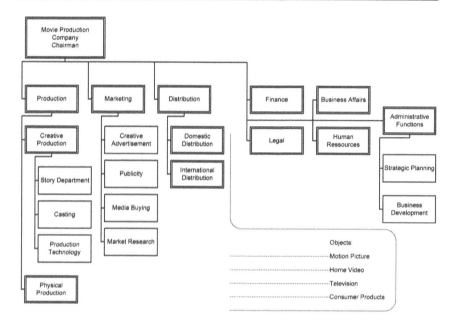

Figure 10: Organizational chart of a major Hollywood movie production company

4.3 Business Process Overview

The main goal of this case study is a detailed description of the movie production process. I will examine the important activities in each phase of the production, investigate the responsibilities and interconnections between the actors involved and describe the milestones at the end of a phase. I will use the Rational Unified Process, a software development process model, as a methodical framework to structure my use case analysis (see Figure 11).

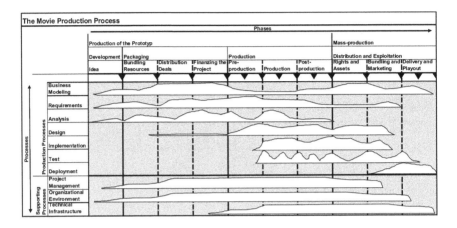

Figure 11: The movie production process

This life cycle model of a movie production project shows the production process divided into different phases: development, packaging, production and distribution/exploitation. The phases consist of various sub-phases or steps. Each phase ends with a milestone, a predefined result, marked as a solid triangle. There can be numerous iterations of each step, especially in the production phases. At the beginning of each process iteration, realistic and verifiable goals for the following period are set and reviewed at the end.

The chart shows the different workloads of the processes during the individual phases. These processes can be divided into production and supporting processes. Production processes are directly linked to the creative steps of shooting a movie. Supporting processes are basically management tasks. The meaning of the processes is described in the following paragraph.

Business modeling:

The business modeling process ensures the overall understanding of the project as a specific product. The primary question is, "What kind of movie will be developed in terms of genre, costs, predicted revenues, franchise opportunities, desired audience, etc.?" All members of the project network have to agree to the business model in order to achieve the common goal.

Requirements:

The requirements are closely linked to the selected business model. In this process the requirements of every project stakeholder have to be set out. In my analysis, the business modeling and requirements processes are handled together.

Analysis:

The analysis process defines the story while observing the requirements. The screenplay is written primarily during this process.

Design:

The design process breaks down the script. The screen actors, the locations, the overall look and the budget of the film are specified. The combination of analysis and design suits my own analysis best.

Implementation:

In the implementation process the different movie components are created, i.e. live action shots are filmed or special effects sequences are rendered. These components are brought together at the end of each iteration. To reduce risks, these prototypes show the end product early on in the production process.

Test:

Early prototypes are screened in the testing process. Observing the requirements of the business model a given quality must be achieved. I will handle implementation and test as a single process.

Deployment:

The deployment process follows production and includes handing over the finished product to the client. The movie created by the production team must meet the buyer's expectations.

Project Management:

This is an important process in movie production. Project management plans both the schedule and the budget. Shooting must also be supervised and controlled. The phases and iterations have to be planned, as well.

Organizational Environment:

The organizational environment process builds up the project network and deals with the requirements of the different stakeholders.

Technical Infrastructure:

In this process the technical infrastructure for shooting the movie, for transmitting data or for the post-production must be defined and set up. This process will take on even greater importance in the future, when movie production switches to digital.

4.4 Development

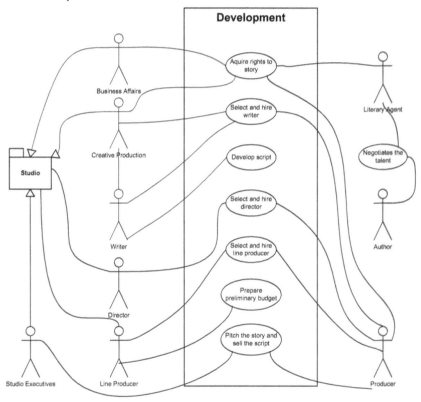

Figure 12: Use cases of the development phase

The primary phase of every movie production project is the development of the idea, involving processes such as business modeling and requirements, analysis, project management and organizational environment (see Figure 12).

The major studios have a story department as part of their creative production department. The creative team evaluates material from the literary marketplace, and determines what to buy and try to develop into a movie.[105] This material might be a book or an early version of a screenplay. Only the literary agent of an author or a very well known entertainment lawyer can offer solicited screenplays to the studio.[106] The studio has a certain budget, not included in the general production budget, set aside for development. This development budget is used to pay the people involved in development and to secure film rights by buying the material. Another alternative is to option the rights to the material for a limited time only. At the end of this period, if the development has not led to a film production, the rights fall back to the author or other rights holder. Ultimately, only around 10% of the material in development is actually produced. This is a rough approximation and each studio has different percentages. The major Hollywood movie production company tends to hold around 220 projects in various stages of active development, a number which is typical for a major studio. In contrast to this, around 14 to 16 movies are released each year. A major studio needs a balance of genres, such as thriller, comedy, or action, throughout the year. Therefore, the studio must strive for both a balanced release slate and quality material in different genres. For the same reason, the creative production department and literary agents both know that they must work with projects in many different genres, and a studio executive might ask for comedy submissions, for example, if that studio was short on comedies. This shows that the production executives, who are among those who decide which projects to abandon and which ones to greenlight (to raise a project from development to production), not only need good knowledge of available literature, but also of market taste. The creative production department must decide what kind of movies the major Hollywood movie production company will to produce. Normally the major Hollywood movie production company looks for a certain number of its movies to have a "popcorn cinema" style, with merchandising abilities and a potential future franchise.[107]

---

[105] Interviewee_2 (2004)
[106] Interviewee_5 (2004)
[107] Interviewee_2 (2004)

Nowadays the marketing department is also involved in the development process.[108] Their market research department assists in predicting project performance with respect to the genre and the package containing the key creative players such as the director, the stars, and the producers. Upon acquisition of material for the film, the powerful creative production department and the marketing department will request a specific producer. They are also involved in choosing the writers, the director and the stars.[109] The bundle of key players is important for the project to become green light. The script has to be in the right form with the right producers, directors and screen actors. For example, "Movie_A" was in development 6 to 8 years before the package was right.[110] You must have a name in the industry and the connections to the decision makers to obtain the right package. That is one reason why talent agencies for writers, screen actors, etc. have become so important in recent years.

The role of the producers has also changed. There used to be only one producer per movie, who supervised the whole project. Nowadays there can be up to ten producers specialized on different tasks. Some producers are just packagers. They have the best connections to studio executives or other investors and collect the money. These packager-producers then have real producers working on the movie for them. If a producer is successful, he often leaves the studio and founds his own production company.[111] These companies normally produce a maximum of three movies a year. The major Hollywood movie production company has contracts with some of these producers and pays them for the right to have the first look at the producer's material. If the major Hollywood movie production company does not like the script or the film, the producer may receive permission to sell it to another studio. A movie is easily greenlighted if a star like Tom Cruise or Steven Spielberg wants to do the movie and the budget is viable. It is therefore quite common when there is a new script to sell that an agent will be careful in selecting which producers to send it to, based on the producer's ability and track record of selling the script to a studio, and then pushing the script from development to production.[112] If the studio accepts the material, they hire their own writers to work out a filmable script. This is a technical form of writing and is often done by writers who are specialized in dialogues

---

[108] Interviewee_6 (2004)
[109] Interviewee_3 (2004)
[110] Interviewee_2 (2004)
[111] Interviewee_3 (2004)
[112] Interviewee_2 (2004)

or action sequences. "Movie_B", for example, was authored by six writers.[113] The writing phase normally takes from six to twelve weeks. Often the director and the producer bring their ideas and input to the writers.[114]

The person truly in charge of the movie is not the producer himself but his line producer.[115] He has to break down the script and prepare a preliminary budget for the movie. With the script written, and the budget and package of key talents finalized, the producer pitches the project to the studio executives. If they decide the movie's business model meets the major Hollywood movie production company's expectations, it gets greenlighted.

The basic process in the development phase is the business modeling and requirements process. In this process the rights to the script are acquired and the script is written. The producer tries to build up a working business model and to sell it to the studio.

In the analysis process, the script is broken down and an initial provisional budget is drawn up.

In the project management process, the activities of the development phase are scheduled and supervised by the producer.

In the organizational environment process, the people involved in the development process are brought together.

The actors responsible and involved in the different activities can be extracted directly from the use case diagram (see Figure 12). The basic artifact in the development phase is the written screenplay. There can be iterations of the development phase, when a project is not greenlighted after its first pitch. Then the script, the involved talents or even the studio might be changed. The milestone of the development phase is the studio green light to produce the movie.

---

[113] Interviewee_3 (2004)
[114] Interviewee_7 (2004)
[115] Interviewee_3 (2004)

4.5 Packaging

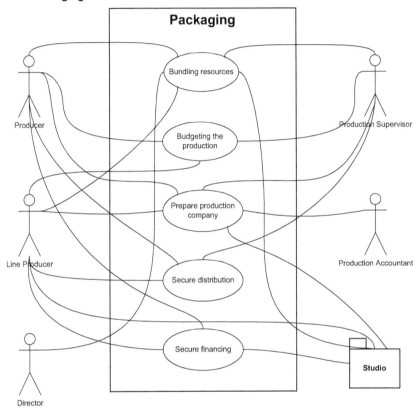

Figure 13: Use cases of the packaging phase

The packaging phase consists of the three basic elements: bundling necessary project resources, securing movie distribution and securing project financing (see Figure 13). The processes involved in these phases are the same as in the development phase: business modeling and requirements, analysis and design, project management and organizational environment.

In this phase work on the script is still in progress. The ideas of the director, the producer and, of course, the studio are built in. The business model is refined and the project budget and schedule can be calculated more precisely. This is an essential step prior to the start of negotiations with financiers and distributors (see Figure 14).

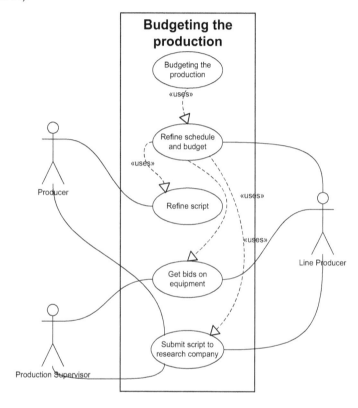

Figure 14: Use cases of budgeting the production

The line producer has to calculate the production costs, including the idea itself, the estimated above-the-line costs for talents as well as the below-the-line costs for technical elements and production staff.[116] An experienced line producer can predict the below-the-line costs very accurately by breaking down the script with a tool like "Movie Magic Budgeting", for example. For some scenes, especially special effects shots, cost estimates are made by research companies. An average major studio

---

[116] Interviewee_4 (2004)

movie costs about US$ 65 million for production and another US$ 35 million for marketing. About 25-30% of the production costs are above-the-line, meaning that US$ 15-20 million go for the cast, as well as the author, director and producer.[117] In addition to that, the post-production costs, especially for visual effects, have to be calculated early on. An example: the very expensive movie "Movie_C" cost around US$ 160 million, with US$ 60 million for post-production alone and of that US$ 35-40 million for about 1000 digital visual effects shots.[118] Once the high costs for special effects and especially those for stars have been negotiated successfully by a talent agency, a studio like the major Hollywood movie production company will have to accept the new market price.[119]

The basic steps in the organizational environment process are set out in the use case "Prepare Production Company" (see Figure 15). In this use case a production company is formed and bank accounts are opened. Furthermore, the company needs to have insurances in place before they can arrange deals with the studio.[120]

---

[117] Interviewee_5 (2004)
[118] Interviewee_3 (2004)
[119] Interviewee_5 (2004)
[120] Interviewee_1 (2004)

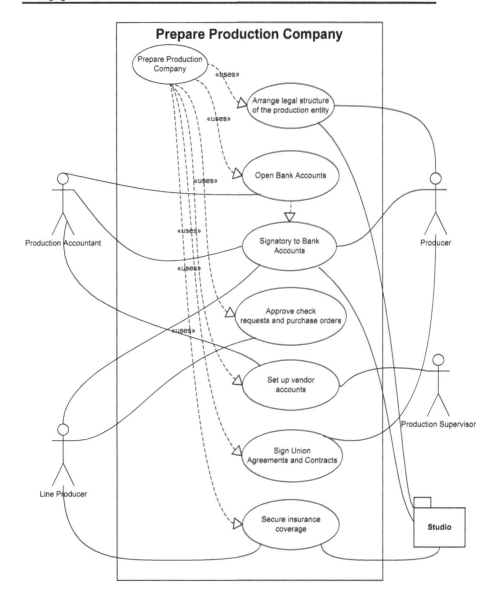

Figure 15: Use cases of preparing the production company

4.5.1   Bundling Resources

A model of one packaging sub-phase is shown in the use case diagram "Bundling Resources" (see Figure 16). As already mentioned in the development phase, it is important to bundle the right package of talents for a given movie. Studios maintain contracts with certain pieces of talent. To make these contracts a worthwhile investment, the studios hope to greenlight movies that are developed by the talent. More importantly, however, is their suitability for the project and of course their availability,[121] hence the studio often bundles external human resources. Crew casting influences the scheduling and, with that, other processes as well. As each star has a certain market power, which is highly important for the outcome of a movie, it is common to schedule the production according to the availability of such key players. Most big studio movies make more than 50% of their total gross overseas. To attract foreign audiences the major Hollywood movie production company sometimes hires screen actors who are stars in their home country. As an example, in "Movie_3" the major Hollywood movie production company contracted a female star from Spain and gained a significantly higher gross there.[122]

The hiring of team members falls into the organizational environment process. Negotiations with stars and other talents also affect business modeling.

Iterations can occur if, for example, the package does not meet the expectations of an investor.

The milestone at the end of the bundling phase is the contractual commitment of key players to the project.

---

[121] Interviewee_2 (2004)
[122] Interviewee_7 (2004)

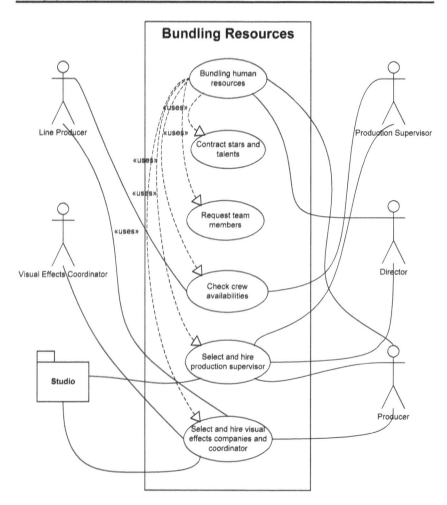

Figure 16: Use cases of bundling resources

4.5.2   Distribution Deals

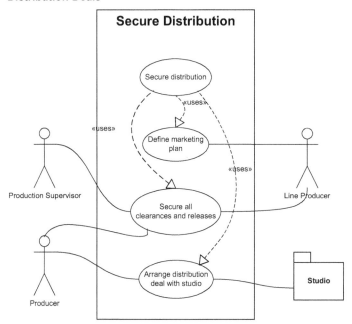

Figure 17: Use cases of securing the distribution

Once the screen actors and other talents like the director are tied to the project, and an elaborated version of the script together with an updated budget and schedule have been bundled, the package for raising money for the production stands. The key activity in this phase is selling the product to a distributor before it has been produced (see Figure 17). In this case the distributor is the major Hollywood movie production company. A few years back, the budget for a major movie could be secured by selling the international distribution rights alone. Today this makes up for only about 50% of the production costs. An independent movie, one in which the money does not come from a major studio, is sold mainly on film markets like the American Film Market (AFM) in Santa Monica or similar events in Toronto, Cannes, Venice or Berlin. Production companies there present the script, the director and the stars and try to sell the distribution rights. Often a foreign distributor like the German distribution company Constantin becomes a co-producer and thus receives the exclusive distribution rights, in this case for Germany.[123] Prominent independently financed movies include the "Lord of the Rings Trilogy".

The activities described above are part of the business modeling process.

This phase will be iterated until most of the rights are sold.

The milestone at the end of this phase is the successful arrangement of distribution deals.

4.5.3 Financing the Project

The phase "financing the project" is similar to the phase "distribution deals", although in the financing phase money is invested, instead of being earned by selling the product in advance. A movie project normally also need to raise money on the capital market. The investors are banks, film funds , media companies or private investors. The recoupment plan supported by the distribution deals throughout the diverse exploitation windows forms the basis for negotiations. To predict the economical outcome of a movie is becoming more and more difficult. No indication can be made until the film is produced or, more accurately, until the opening weekend grosses are published. However, the investors must make their decisions solely on the basis of the package.

The following processes take place in this phase: business modeling, project management and organizational environment.

Iterations are necessary if preconditions change during the packaging process.

Securing the project financing concludes this phase and is as such the last milestone before the start of production.

---

[123] Interviewee_12 (2004)

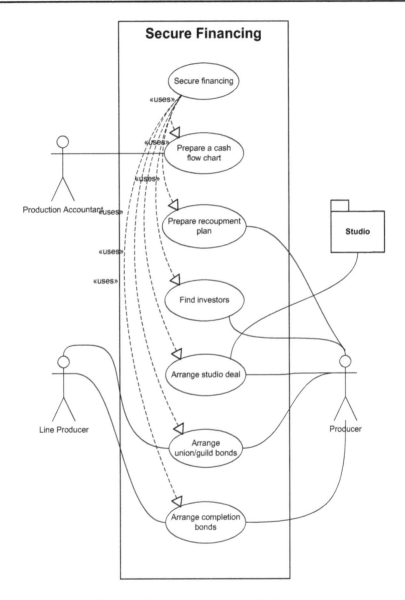

Figure 18: Use cases of securing the financing

4.6   Production

There are numerous activities in the three production phases. Use cases are assigned to different production and supporting processes to keep the diagrams clear.

4.6.1   Pre-production

The pre-production phase begins with the studio's commitment to making the movie. Normally, a release date will already have been set. At this stage the production company secures everything required to begin shooting the film. The following use case diagrams give an overview of these steps.

For the pre-production phases, the involved processes – business modeling and requirements, analysis and design, implementation and test, project management, organizational environment and technical infrastructure – are modeled in separate diagrams.

Iterations in the pre-production phase are normal. For some scenes they can continue until principal photography is finished.

The pre-production milestone is reached once preparations have advanced far enough for principal photography to start.

Business modeling and requirements:

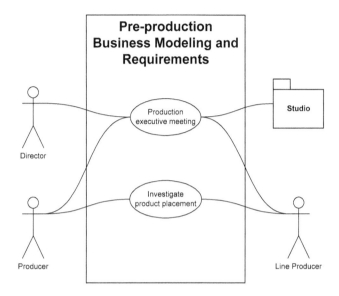

Figure 19: Use cases of the pre-production: business modeling and requirements

In pre-production phase the business model is adapted once again (see Figure 19). During the pre-production of "Movie_C" for example, the conception of related TV series, video games and the added-value DVD were strategically planned and assigned.[124] Some movies are made within ten months. A video game production takes at least 18 to 24 months, so the major Hollywood movie production company has to start the production of a movie-related game during the pre-production phase of the movie. The costs for the production of a video game run about US$ 4-5 million plus another US$ 10-15 million for marketing. In a few years, production costs will reach US$ 8 million with a production team of 50 to 75 people. The production processes of movies and videogames will converge. Video game producers will start hiring writers and storyboard artists for their games. Furthermore, digital elements like the 3D models used for virtual characters in movies can be used for video games production as well, calling for the video game artists to be integrated into the movie production process as early on as possible. The US market for video games is about

---

[124] Interviewee_7 (2004)

US$ 8 billion.[125] By comparison, the US movie industry grosses about US$ 8.5 billion in theatrical exhibition.[126] The mobile gaming market should not be underestimated, either. Before long the US market will grow from US$ 700 million to an estimated US$ 5 billion.

When refining the business model, executives also decide on possible product placement deals in the movie as well as the recently established product placements and advertisements in video games.[127]

Analysis and design:

In the analysis and design process, the script is rewritten and refined several times before the scenes and their time and money requirements match the shooting schedule and budget (see Figure 20). In the meantime the look of the film must be specified, closely coupled with decisions on where and how each scene should be shot, be it on a studio soundstage, on location or even in components, meaning the screen actors stand in front of a green (or blue) screen with the background plates added later. Figuring out how and where to shoot the scenes and calculating how expensive they might be is a time-intensive undertaking. These complex decisions must be properly optimized under the constraints of time and money.[128] Even in the case of a movie of the major Hollywood movie production company, executives calculate whether to build the sets and shoot in their own studios or to go elsewhere. For example, in Los Angeles a grip (a grip prepares rigs and mounts lights) costs US$ 27 per hour. In Canada the same service can be obtained for about US$ 14 per hour.[129] "Movie_C" was shot in Prague, where the costs for building the sets were five times lower than in the US. Furthermore, the sets could remain in place for the production of a TV series, which would not have been possible at the area of the studio. Nevertheless, other aspects had to be taken into consideration as well. A typical shooting day in Prague lasts from 7 a.m. to 7 p.m. with a five-day week. In Los Angeles a typical shooting day can have 18 hours with a six-day week.[130]

---

[125] Interviewee_11 (2004)
[126] Interviewee_10 (2004)
[127] Interviewee_11 (2004)
[128] Interviewee_7 (2004)
[129] Interviewee_4 (2004)
[130] Interviewee_7 (2004)

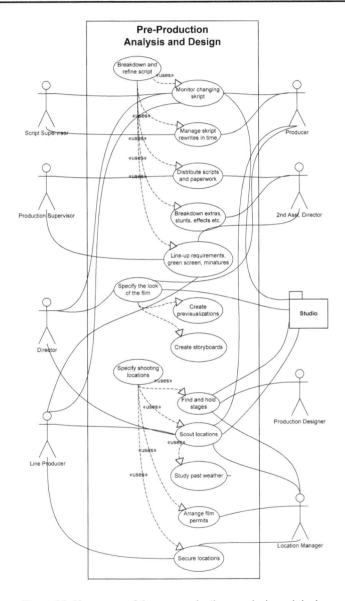

Figure 20: Use cases of the pre-production: analysis and design

The lot of the major Hollywood movie production company is very well equipped. It is an industrialized infrastructure supporting the whole process of the physical production. Producers of big studio movies, independent movies or TV productions not only rent the soundstages and back lot locations (the outside locations in the studio's compound) but also electrical equipment and power, lights, construction, crafts, catering, grips, transportation, parking, air conditioning, security, emergency services, telecommunications, props and costumes, as well as the post-production facilities, ADR (automated dialog replacement), foley (sound design), music stages, mixing suites, etc. The major Hollywood movie production company does not have its own animation studio. So it has to subcontract other companies to produce its animation.[131] Alone the pre-production phase of "Movie_C" cost around US$ 10 million.[132]

Implementation and test:

The initial producing tasks are carried out in the implementation and test process (see Figure 21). Additionally, cast preparation activities like rehearsals or training, the wardrobe and props (properties) have to be selected, rented or produced. Also, the sets need to be built and decorated. The director and producer approve every item.

---

[131] Interviewee_2 (2004)
[132] Interviewee_7 (2004)

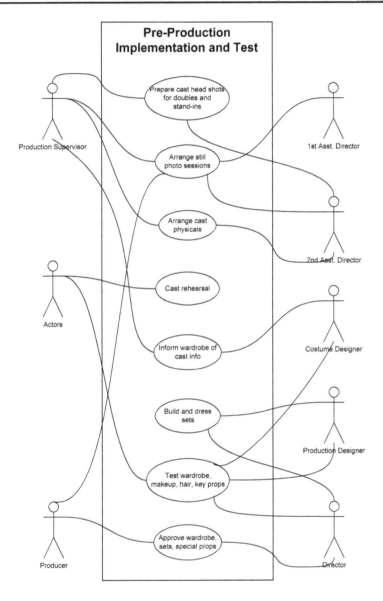

Figure 21: Use cases of the pre-production: implementation and test

Project Management:

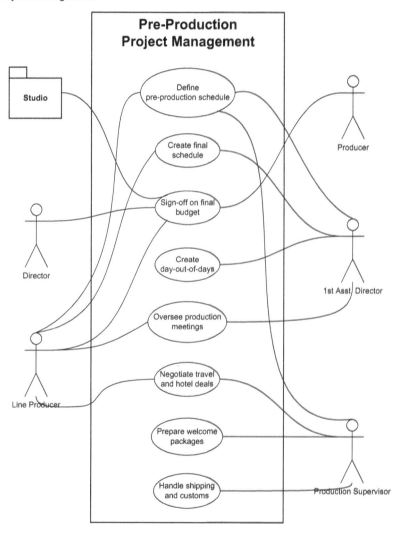

Figure 22: Use cases of the pre-production: project management

The project management process consists basically of scheduling and budgeting activities. In pre-production the script has to be broken down to create the final schedule to write day-out-of-days, concise information on which screen actors are needed on which days and for which tasks. A positive relationship between the people involved is a huge asset in a movie production; preparing little welcome packages at the start of the project can foster this.[133]

Organizational environment:

The main concern in the organizational environment process of the pre-production phase is the hiring of cast and crew (see Figure 23). This use case diagram gives an overview of the key players involved, divided into screen actors and crew. The second diagram of the organizational environment process shows the use cases essential for running operations (see Figure 24). It should not go unmentioned that the US movie industry is very strongly unionized. The importance of forming good relationships with the unions and observing and obeying their regulations must not be underestimated. This is also addressed in the organizational environment process, e.g. there must be at least two union employees working on the set.[134]

---

[133] Interviewee_4 (2004)
[134] Interviewee_1 (2004)

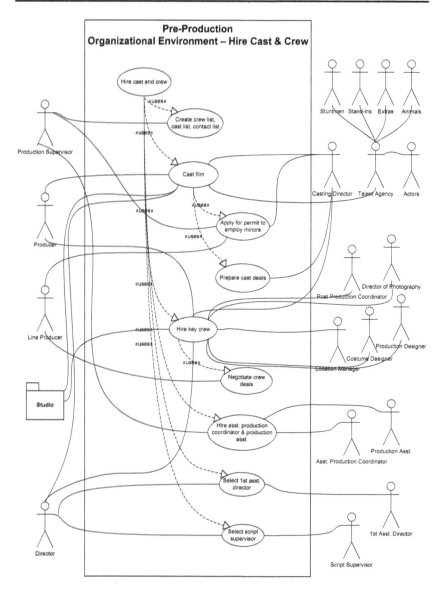

Figure 23: Use cases of the pre-production: organizational environment (A)

Figure 24: Use cases of the pre-production: organizational environment (B)

Technical infrastructure:

Production can rely on the studio's technical infrastructure when shooting on soundstages in the studio of the major Hollywood movie production company. Nevertheless, the equipment and the facilities have to be secured and negotiated (see Figure 25).

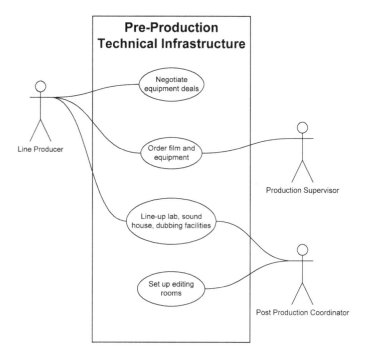

Figure 25: Use cases of the pre-production: technical infrastructure

4.6.2   Physical Production

The actual filming of scenes takes place in the production phase. In addition to creative tasks performed by the artists in this phase, management has to ensure that the production process runs smoothly, with steady progress in accordance with the plan developed in the pre-production phase.

The involved processes – implementation and test, project management and organizational environment – are again modeled in separate use case diagrams.

Iterations take place during the production phase, too. Scenes are re-shot until the desired level of quality is achieved. Even after the cutting process in the post-production phase the team must sometimes be called back for so-called pick-up shots, the reshooting of selected scenes.

The production phase milestone is reached once the last scene has been successfully shot.

The following diagram shows an overview of the physical production (see Figure 26). The Director of Photography is directly connected with and responsible for photography. He also oversees the lighting for the scenes, which, together with the makeup of the screen actors, their costumes and props, play as important a role as the location of the shoot, be it on location or on a soundstage.

The effects can be divided into practical effects and visual effects. Practical effects happen on set in front of the camera – for example the usage of forced perspective or mirrors to simulate dimensions. The following are examples of visual effects: process photography means the screen actors play in front of a projection of a background movie. Process photography was typically used for dialogue scenes in moving cars, instead of mounting a camera on the car or towing the car on a trailer. Nowadays this technique is often replaced by greenscreen compositing, where the background plate is later exchanged digitally. Models and miniatures are still used for effects shots, even though computer generated imagery (CGI) is becoming more and more powerful and prevalent, as is the creation of digital characters animated by hand or by motion capturing of real screen actors.

The following use cases concentrate on principal photography, the shooting basic scenes with the screen actors, on set or on location. Other elements of the physical production are often shot by second or third production units.

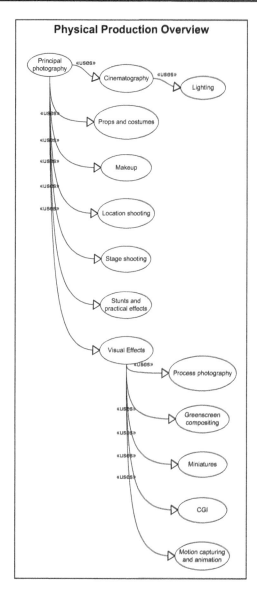

Figure 26: Overview of the elements of principal photography

Implementation and test:

In the implementation and test process the director directs the screen actors and works closely together with the director of photography (DP) to shoot the scenes. A team of specialized people are involved and stand by. The DP normally supervises an A-camera crew and a B-camera crew, consisting of a camera operator who operates the camera angles and moves, and an assistant camera operator who operates the focus. A and B cameras are often mounted on a dolly or crane. The C camera as a steadycam (a camera carried by the camera operator) is becoming more and more important for dynamic movement in the picture. The cameras are moved by dolly grips and crane operators. On-set sound is recorded by the sound mixer; the boom operator holds the microphone attached to a long pole over the set,. The gaffer and the best boy (or nowadays called the chief lighting technician and his assistant) set up the lights for the scene. The set decorator and his people from the art department prepare the set and check it for each scene. The costume supervisor, makeup artists and the property master stand by in case they are needed, making sure that the screen actors look the same in each scene. The script supervisor has to make sure that the scenes are shot as written in the script. The photos taken by the still photographer help keep an overview of the continuity between scenes that belong together. Furthermore, there are a number of grips, electricians, cable men, drivers, craft services and a variety of assistants helping on set; and last but not least, security and emergency services. On a normal day there are from 50 to 200 people involved in shooting.

The studio executives involved in the project supervise the production by reviewing the dailies, the scenes produced on a particular day.[135] The first two weeks of a production are crucial. The dailies mirror whether the team can work together or changes have to be made. Do the director of photography and the screen actors meet their expectations? Are wardrobes, hair or set decoration suitable for the movie? The first two weeks can be seen as a kind of prototyping.[136] While watching the dailies, the executives also check whether the movie meets certain requirements, such as desired ratings. Do the scenes involve nudity, explicit language or violence, and if so, can they be cut out for special airline or television releases?[137] It is still

---

[135] Interviewee_4 (2004)
[136] Interviewee_7 (2004)
[137] Interviewee_4 (2004)

common for the dailies to be copied onto VHS tape and sent to the executives. By way of illustration, the dailies of "Movie_D" produced in New Zealand arrived in Los Angeles with a five day delay.[138] Screening the dailies can also give a first glimpse at the potential market value of the movie. In addition, executives use scientific tools like "Silverscreener" to predict movie performance, but experience shows that these tools are not as accurate as relying on their common sense while screening the production.[139]

The following use case diagram gives a short overview of the on-set responsibilities during the implementation and test process (see Figure 27).

[138] Interviewee_7 (2004)
[139] Interviewee_6 (2004)

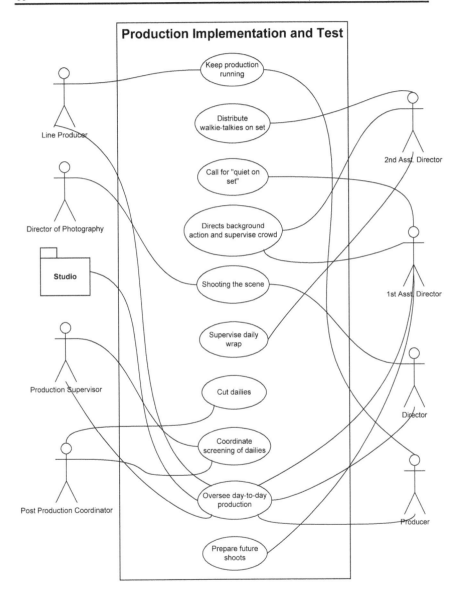

Figure 27: Use cases of the production: implementation and test

Project management:

The most important tasks in the project management process are scheduling, budgeting and communications.[140] The schedule must be adapted continuously. Changes may occur because set-building is not finished, scenes have to reshot for artistic or quality reasons, or simply the weather did not allow a certain scene to be shot.

If half a day is missed during production, the director and the producer have to shorten the script and cut out other scenes. The other possibility is to ask the creative production department to invest extra money. The daily production costs for a big movie with a total budget of around US$ 100 million are between US$ 250,000 and 300,000 per day when shooting at the studio. On location these costs are slightly higher.[141] The line producer has to supervise the budget. He explains to the executives and the finance department whether the production is on schedule and within budget.[142] These reports are due on a weekly basis at a minimum.[143] A producer must have common sense and the ability to make decisions right away to keep the production rolling. Under normal circumstances, no one on set will question his decisions. Quite often the producer has to balance artistic and economic requests.[144] The production services department has to be flexible in fulfilling such requests. They have to plan the logistics and locations while serving various productions with changing needs.[145]

The first of the following two use case diagrams shows the project management tasks during principal photography. The second diagram focuses on budget and schedule controlling (see Figure 28 and Figure 29).

---

[140] Interviewee_1 (2004)
[141] Interviewee_3 (2004)
[142] Interviewee_4 (2004)
[143] Interviewee_7 (2004)
[144] Interviewee_3 (2004)
[145] Interviewee_1 (2004)

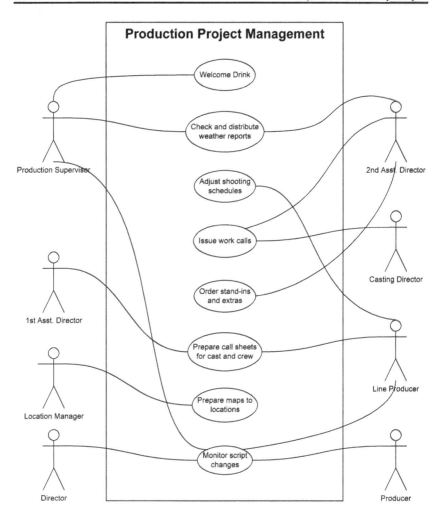

Figure 28: Use cases of the production: project management (A)

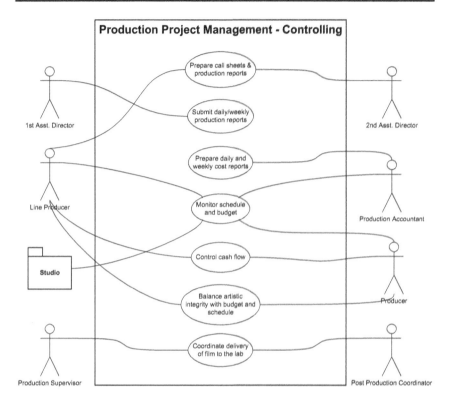

Production Project Management - Controlling

1st Asst. Director

2nd Asst. Director

Line Producer

Production Accountant

Studio

Producer

Production Supervisor

Post Production Coordinator

Prepare call sheets & production reports

Submit daily/weekly production reports

Prepare daily and weekly cost reports

Monitor schedule and budget

Control cash flow

Balance artistic integrity with budget and schedule

Coordinate delivery of film to the lab

Figure 29: Use cases of the production: project management (B)

Organizational environment:

The large array of people specialized on various tasks on set help to free up the director, allowing him to focus on the shooting. The following diagram shows the responsibilities of the first and second assistant directors (see Figure 30).

Close cooperation with unions and guilds is essential in the organizational environment process. In addition, the press is invited to visit the set as an early marketing strategy. The entertainment industry papers like Hollywood Reporter or

Daily Variety are paid by the major Hollywood movie production company to publish articles about movies in production to generate interest (see Figure 31).[146]

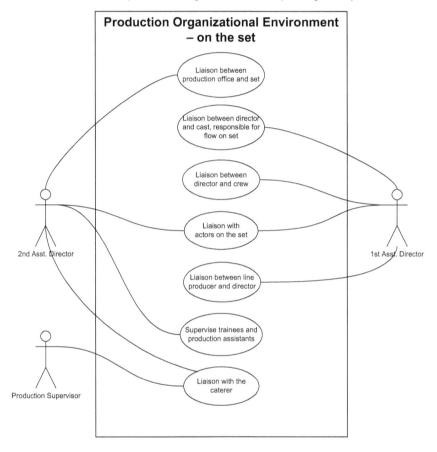

Figure 30: Use cases of the production: organizational environment (A)

[146] Interviewee_4 (2004)

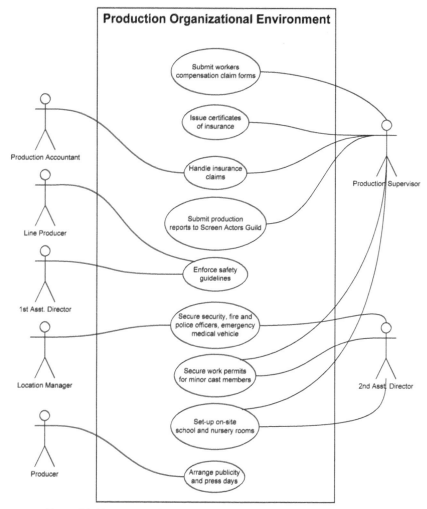

Figure 31: Use cases of the production: organizational environment (B)

4.6.3   Post-production

In the post-production phase the raw film material is cut, and the different elements such as sounds, dialogues, music and digital effects are assembled. Similar to the production phase, there is a strict schedule, which must be adhered in order to meet the date set for the start of distribution. The processes involved are implementation and test, deployment, project management and organizational environment. As in the previous production phases, these are modeled in separate use case diagrams.

The post-production phase is characterized by continuous efforts to ensure the desired quality level is met. Some use cases must be iterated many times until this level is achieved.

The milestone at the end of the post-production phase is the delivery of the completed movie to the studio and the start of distribution with the premiere.

Implementation and test:

In the implementation and test process, the film is cut and continuously screened by the director, the producer and the studio. If the film is shot on 35mm celluloid, the material is first digitized for the cutting process and the entire post-production phase.[147] However, digital filming will soon become more popular, and digital technology itself will continue to improve.[148] "Spiderman 2" was the first movie edited in the forthcoming studio standard 4k, which uses a picture resolution of 4096x3112 pixels.[149] The post-production phase will become even more important as the volume of digitally created images and screen actors or creatures animated by motion control increases further.[150] Furthermore, the requisite technology will become cheaper.[151]

It is sometimes necessary to arrange pickup-shots if missing or imperfect scenes are discovered during the cutting process. In such cases, the team can decide whether digital methods might be an option or if a re-shoot is faster and cheaper.[152]

The movie credits are compiled in the implementation and test process. Some of the credits are negotiated in advance within the contracts with the talents, but most of the

---

[147] Interviewee_12 (2004)
[148] Interviewee_4 (2004)
[149] Interviewee_12 (2004)
[150] Interviewee_4 (2004)
[151] Interviewee_6 (2004)
[152] Interviewee_3 (2004)

credits are controlled by tremendously powerful guilds, such as the Screen Actors Guild (SAG), the Directors Guild of America (DGA) or the Writers Guild of America (WGA).[153]

The following diagram is the first part of an overview of use cases required in the implementation and test process (see Figure 32).

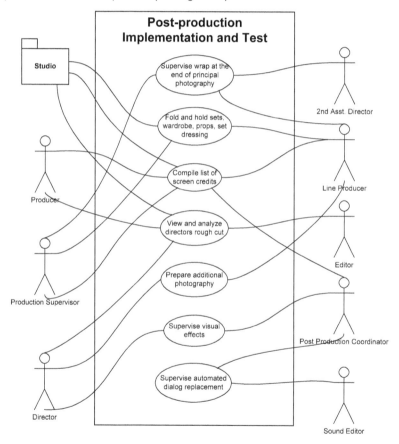

Figure 32: Use cases of the post-production: implementation and test (A)

---

[153] Interviewee_5 (2004)

Aside from special effects, the sounds and music have to be produced. Film music is a key element in transporting emotions intended for a scene to the audience. The major Hollywood movie production company spent US$ 3 million on the music for "Movie_C".[154]

The major Hollywood movie production company often arranges test screenings for a selected audience to study their reactions and to gain valuable information on to how the director and editor might improve the final cut. Both the studio, as the main investor, and the producer have the right to decide on the final cut if the editor and director are not in agreement with their ideas.

---

[154] Interviewee_3 (2004)

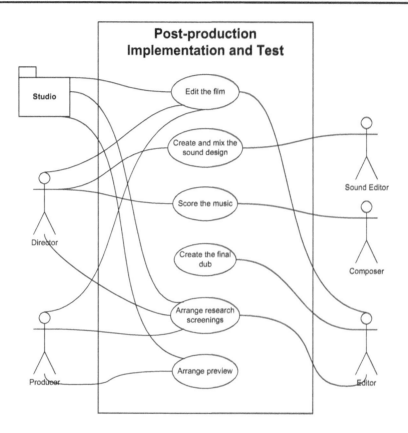

Figure 33: Use cases of the post-production: implementation and test (B)

Deployment:

In the deployment process the production team turns the material over to the studio (see Figure 34). As mentioned above, the studio analyses the potential market value of the product very carefully to assess the likelihood of recouping the money invested in the product. In the deployment process, the movie release is prepared, and the necessary marketing campaigns are initiated.[155]

---

[155] Interviewee_8/Interviewee_9 (2004)

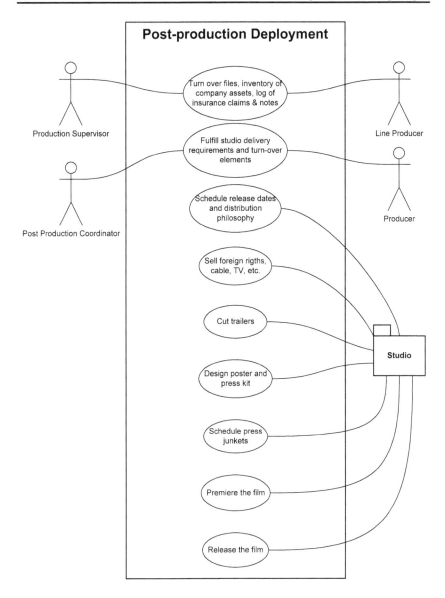

Figure 34: Use cases of the post-production: deployment

Project management:

The project management basically involves scheduling of the pre-production and the supervision of the associated tasks (see Figure 35). Many post-production activities are assigned to specialized companies. For example, the digital shots of "Movie_C" were outsourced to George Lucas' Industrial Light and Magic by the major Hollywood movie production company, and one person was given the task of supervising the required daily transfer of data between the major Hollywood movie production company and the special effects company in Northern California.[156]

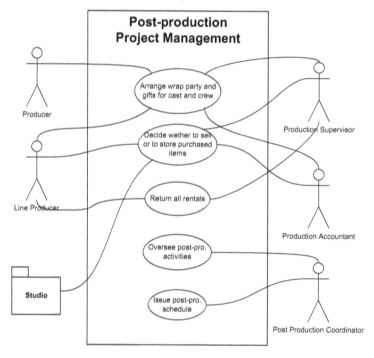

Figure 35: Use cases of the post-production: project management

---

Organizational environment:

Finally, the production office has to be closed down after the deployment of the completed movie, as can be seen in the following use case diagram of the organizational environment process (see Figure 36).

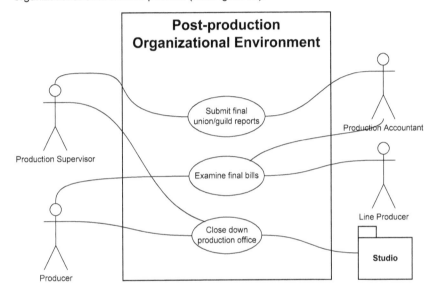

Figure 36: Use cases of the post-production: organizational environment

The subsequent phase, distribution and exploitation, is not a part of my research area.

5 Reference Modeling of an Integrated Movie Production System

In the previous Chapter, the descriptive case study analysis, I used my own observations and interviews with executives at the major Hollywood movie production company, as well as a literature review to describe the movie production process in detail. The responsibilities of the main actors involved in the production process are shown in the use cases. These diagrams form the foundation and the requirements for my design of a reference model of the movie production system.

The following Chapter uses the approach explained in Chapter 3.2 to construct the reference model.[157] The classification of the reference model and the modeling process are specified in that Chapter. The underlying framework for the reference model is discussed in greater detail in Chapter 4.3. The reference model represents the organizational architecture, data architecture, application architecture, technical architecture and information architecture.

5.1 Organizational Architecture: Departments, Actors and Roles

The case study analysis of Chapter 4 describes the main actors involved in the production process and their use cases. This Chapter will specify more precisely the people involved in a movie production. In a major Hollywood production, 400 to 800 involved actors are quite common.[158] These actors are organized into departments. Furthermore, specific tasks and occasionally entire departments are outsourced to external experts or specialized companies. As described in Chapter 2, when building up the network for a motion picture production, reputation and experience are the main factors enabling producers to decide on the suitability of people or companies for the network. Therefore, most of the players are chosen either from within the

---

[157] See also Tzouvaras (2003), pp. 123, Dietze (2004) pp. 10, Remus (2002) pp. 7

[158] The Internet Movie Database lists the cast and crew of movie productions. These lists normally comprise the people mentioned in the end credits of a movie. Not everyone who participated in the production team is credited. In King Kong (Universal Pictures et al., 2005) about 400 people were credited, due to this date 4 people are listed as "uncredited", see IMDB (2005a). In Star Wars 3 (Lucasfilm, 2005) about 550 people were credited, 50 were not, see IMDB (2005b). In Lord of the Rings 3 (New Line Cinema et al., 2003) about 730 people were credited, 20 were not, see IMDB (1993). In Titanic (20th Century Fox et al., 1997) about 1300 people were credited, 150 were not, see IMDB (1997). And in Jurassic Park (Universal Pictures et al., 1993) about 500 people were credited, 50 were not, see IMDB (2003).

studio or from a pool of specialists for certain elements of the movie production process who have acquired a positive track record for the tasks at hand.[159]

The following model (Figure 37) gives an example of one possible configuration of a movie production network. The model shows the departments attached to the network. It consists of three concentric circles divided into three sectors. The inner circle describes the departments that are most likely staffed by studio departments. The middle circle describes the pool of independent companies or individuals who are repeatedly chosen as members of a production network. The outer circle describes assignments that can be recruited from the market. I organized the departments by looking at the essence of their specific jobs in the movie production and by dividing them into business tasks, creative tasks or technical tasks. The data processed in this model is condensed from the case study in Chapter 4 and from my own analysis of a number of credit lists.

As can be deduced from the model, great market entry barriers exist for new competitors wanting to join a production network. The producer is always faced with the decision of whether to choose departments from within the studio or to fall back on the pool. The pool plays a decisive role in the movie industry. Even big studios like the major Hollywood movie production company can not fulfill all the producers' needs. For this reason specialized independent companies are frequently chosen for specific tasks.

---

[159] See Picker (2001), pp. 54.

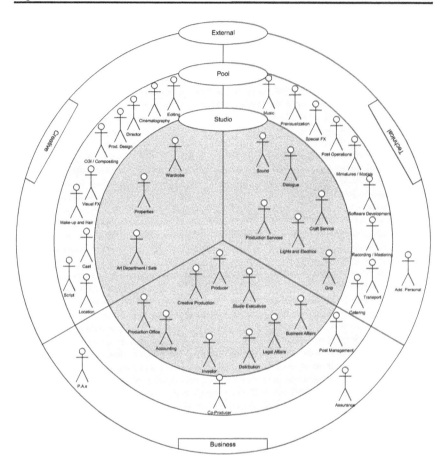

Figure 37: Actor network overview

In the following paragraph I will describe the different departments and organize them into three sectors: business, creative and technical. I point out the responsibilities of the actors within the departments and look at the formation process in the production network.[160]

---

[160] For a description of movie production actors see e.g. IMDB (2005c)

5.1.1 Business Sector:

Producer:

The producer is the orchestrator of the production network and responsible for the production. Although his decisions certainly affect creative and technical issues while supporting the directors' needs, his domain is the business and legal part of the movie production. The producer is the head of the production office. In a studio-driven movie, the studio often employs the producer and the production office. But it is also possible for an independent producer to be hired from the pool to produce a studio movie or a movie for which the producer holds the rights to a specific idea. A producer normally supervises different projects in various stages.

Co-Producer:

As production tasks are diverse, the producer engages specialized co-producers who concentrate on individual production tasks. These co-producers are chosen from the pool by the producer to support the production. There are numerous job titles associated with the various production activities, such as executive producer, associate producer or creative producer. I subsume them under the generic term of "co-producer". An executive producer is responsible for elements concerning development, financing or production of the movie but is generally not involved in the technical realization. An associate producer is responsible for some of the production activities under the supervision of the producer and is sometimes credited as a co-producer. Finally, a creative producer is involved exclusively in creative aspects of the movie production.

Production Office:

Aside from the production manager, key personnel in the production office are the production manager and the line producer. The production manager or unit production manager is part of the upper management and reports directly to the producer. His responsibilities are the below-the-line costs and he supervises the time frame and budgets of all departments. The line producer's responsibilities are similar. He coordinates the day-to-day production and the physical aspects of the film. He breaks down the script, defines a schedule and a budget and controls their compliance. Other titles commonly used for these assignments are production supervisor and production coordinator. In general, the jobs of production manager or line producer of a movie production are more likely to be allocated to an experienced studio employee than someone from the pool. The line producer works on only one project at a time.

Accounting:

The accounting department is responsible for the execution of all financial transactions. The accountants supervise the budgets for different divisions such as set and construction costs, employee paychecks, etc. In general, the accounting department is based within the studio.

Studio Departments:

(Studio Executives, Creative Production, Legal Affairs, and Business Affairs) During different stages of the production various studio departments are involved, e.g. creative production, legal and business affairs. I subsume them together with the responsible studio executives under the classification of "studio departments". The executives work closely together with the producer to design and to supervise the movie as a working business model for the studio. For this reason, the studio departments are sorted into the business sector even though the creative production department has close interdependence with the creative side of the production. In a major Hollywood studio it is not very common for individual functions from these departments to be outsourced to experts from the pool.

Distribution:

The distributor is a business actor in the production network. He is involved in the development process from the early stages on to design a business model for the movie. In a studio-driven production the distributor is normally the studio's own distribution company. To share the immense risk of an expensive production, selling the foreign rights to another studio's distribution company, for example, is common practice. Later in the process further content rights are sold to other distributors like home entertainment or pay-TV and free-to-air. A major studio owns access to every channel, allowing them to exploit these rights in-house or to sell them within their pool. If a computer game is supposed to accompany the movie release, the distribution deals influence the production network. External cinemas are included in the distribution department as recipients of a specific movie format and their requirements are incorporated in the production process.

Investor:

A major studio usually acts as a financing distributor. As such, the investor is in many cases equivalent to the distributor. In addition to the studio, other investors like financial institutions or public film funds may participate in the movie production. They join the network from within the pool.

Insurance:

Completion bonds or other typical forms of insurance can be obtained on the external market, although some insurance companies have specialized products designed for the movie industry. Normally a studio selects their partners from within the pool.

Post-Production Management:

In many cases a large portion of the post-production activities are outsourced to specialized post-production companies. These are often more experienced and better equipped for a specific required task than the internal studio facilities. The post-production management department communicates the business interfaces to these independent companies. They are loosely coupled subcontractors within the production network and have their own organization. The main actors here are the general management of the post-production company, the executive in charge of production and the post-production supervisor. They are responsible for overall post-production and supervise compliance with the requirements of the producer and director. Even though the producer is categorized in business sector, some of his tasks are also closely aligned with the creative sector. In this area selected companies usually come from the pool based on a positive track record with respect to the quality of their work and their ability to react adequately to changing requirements, successfully completing their workload on a tight schedule.

Production Assistants:

A production network is often filled with numerous production assistants (PA) throughout every sector fulfilling a diversity of little jobs with more or less responsibility. Most PAs can be engaged from outside because these jobs are unspecific and uncritical.

5.1.2 Creative Sector:

Director:

The director heads the physical production. Every creative aspect underlies his vision and control, closely coordinated with the producer's and the studio's position. Because of his role as the main creative actor, he gives the final product a very specific character. For this reason he will be selected into the production network from within the pool and based on his earlier work. The director communicates with the screen actors and the various creative and technical departments. He is supported by the 1st and 2nd assistant directors.

Script:

A studio buys the rights to a story from a known literary agent who represents an external author. The studio assigns one or more of their writers to elaborate a script. The script forms the basis of the entire production and is continuously adapted or improved. The script supervisor monitors the production progress and any occurring script changes.

Cinematography:

The director works closely together with the director of photography (DP or cinematographer) to work out the shot compositions for each scene, giving it the desired expressive character. The director of photography carries the overall creative responsibility for every aspect of recording the scene. He is in charge of the camera operators in his department and instructs the lighting department to obtain the desired light for a scene. The director of photography often teams up with the same camera operators. Moreover a director often works with the same DP, when both of them have found a common mode of communication. It is important that the DP understands the vision of the director and is able to realize this vision in the film. The cinematography department is assigned from within the pool.

Editing:

The editor must have abilities similar to the DP and be able to understand the director's vision. His job is to impart the film with suspense and rhythm by cutting and reconstructing the raw material in a manner that effectively supports the storytelling. Consequently, as with the director of photography, a director often works with the same editor who is assigned to the production network from within the pool.

Production Design:

The production design department elaborates the visual appearance of the movie. Supported by his concept artists and storyboard artists, the production designer develops the overall look in cooperation with the director and the art director. The art director is the head of the art department and is responsible for the artists and craftsmen who build the sets. These artists are studio employees or are selected from the pool.

Art Department / Sets:

The art department builds filmable sets developed by the set designer in accordance with the artwork of the production design department. As in the production design department, the artists are normally chosen from within the pool. I assign the department into the creative sector. The department's staff, like carpenters or painters, is generally studio employees.

Location:

The location manager and his location scouts have the task of finding and managing real life locations where the desired look of a scene described by the production designer can be achieved and the necessary logistics of a film crew can be provided. This job is often assigned to an experienced pool member or a specialized company with access to a catalogue of potential locations.

Cast:

Head of the cast department is the casting director. He is specialized on selecting the most suitable screen actor for a speaking role and supports the director and producer in this step. Both the casting director and the cast are selected from within the pool.

Costumes:

The costume designer oversees the design, the selection and the creation of the wardrobe. The costume designer, like most other artists, is selected from within the pool. A major Hollywood studio has a costume and a property storehouse and employs tailors or textile artists.

Property:

The property department is responsible for the fitting and decoration of sets and screen actors with properties (props). The property master oversees the selection and construction of the properties whereas the set dressing coordinator oversees the sets. Again, the artists are often chosen from within the pool.

Make-up and hair:

The make-up and hair department is responsible for the appearance of the screen actors on set. There are specialized firms in the pool that offer these services.

Visual Effects:

The visual effects department designs and realizes scenes that include image alteration in post-production or which are truly digitally generated scenes. These frequently very complex scenes are sometimes outsourced by the director and producer to the visual effects department, which is a small production company in itself, including actors such as a visual effects producer, an art director, an editor, etc. They are responsible for the implementation of their assigned scenes in accordance with the ideas of the director. Often the visual effects departments are specialized in specific areas based on their experience or unique software systems. They are chosen from within the pool.

CGI / Compositing:

The CGI and compositing department is a creative department in which I subsume different digital production elements and production steps. The elements are generally declared as post-production activities and are often outsourced. 3D models are created and animated in this department, 2D graphic elements like background plates are created and the individual elements are finally rendered, lighted and composited. The post-production supervisor oversees the department's activities in collaboration with the director and the producer. Actors or specialized companies for these tasks are selected from within the pool.

5.1.3 Technical Sector:
Sound:

The sound department is responsible for the creation and recording of the sounds assigned to specific actions in a scene. Music and dialogue are separate departments. The sound department fulfils tasks like on set sound recording, artificial sound creation and recording, and foley, the replacement and exaggeration of incidental sound effects. The typical actors are artists, recordists, mixers and assistants. A major Hollywood studio has several sound stages and employs specialists for these tasks.

Dialogue:

The dialogue department is, like foley, a special subdivision of the sound department. The dialogue department is responsible for automated dialogue replacement and also employs recordists and mixers. The dialogue department is typically selected from the studio's resources.

Music:

Due to its similarities with other sound departments I assign the music department to the technical sector, even though the work of the composer is truly creative. The music department is responsible for writing and recording the score and works closely together with the director and producer. The music department comprises the composer and his various assistants like orchestrators or scoring engineers and the recording and mixing technicians. The composer and his team are selected from within the pool, whereas the technicians are basically studio employees.

Post Operations:

The post operations department combines aspects of the technical infrastructure necessary for the post-production activities. The post operations department is responsible for the data transfer and the production network. Depending on whether the post-production activities are outsourced or done by the studio, the post operations department is chosen from within the pool or from the studio.

Previsualization and Video Assist:

The previsualization and video assist department is responsible for the analysis of certain, oftentimes complicated and effect driven scenes. The director hires this department to present him quick, possible scene implementations. The previsualization department often creates and edits small proposals using simple 3D modeling software or game engines to simulate camera angles in action scenes in a fast and cheap manner. These presentations can be used on set to align the camera settings. Using digital cameras, video assist engineers can easily present the recorded image to the director for comparison to the already worked out previsualization scene. These specialized engineers are chosen from within the pool.

Special Effects:

The special effects department is responsible for the on-set special effects to be recorded directly by the cameras. This is in contrast to the visual effects department, which processes single images in post-production. Numerous specialized companies offer a diversity of special effects like pyrotechnics, snow and ice or process photography. These experts are chosen from within the pool.

Miniatures / Models:

The miniatures and models department creates all sorts of miniatures to be filmed separately or with the forced perspective technique on set. Specialized firms from within the pool execute these simultaneously technical and creative tasks.

Recording / Mastering:

The recording and mastering department is a technical post-production department, responsible for the overall look and color timing of the film. Color timing is the adjustment process in post-production to give the individually shot scenes a consistent appearance. If the movie is recorded on film, the department supervises the scanning process. At the end of post-production work, the recording and mastering department oversees the transformation back to film. Specialized firms selected from within the pool fulfill these technical tasks.

Software Development:

The software development department serves the post-production departments in creating innovative tools for diverse applications. These departments are outsourced to experts from within the pool.

Production Services:

The production services department subsumes technical studio facilities like craft services or greensmen. In a studio production these services are normally done with studio resources.

Lights / Electrics:

The lights and electrics department works closely together with the director of photography to light the scene in the way the director has envisioned. In a studio production the lights and electrics department is made up of studio employees.

Grip:

The grip department is responsible for rigging the scaffolding, lights and shields, handling the dolly and techno crane. These technicians are generally studio employees.

Craft Service:

The craft service department is responsible for catering, as well as for cleaning up the set. The craft service department is a unionized and studio-based department. The various activities have developed historically.

Transport:

The transportation department is responsible for the transport of crew and equipment to the different sets. A major Hollywood studio has their own transportation department but also uses companies from the pool.

Catering:

The catering department serves food and drinks to the production crew. The caterer is often chosen from the pool.

Additional Personnel:

Teachers, nurses or security personnel are subsumed as additional personnel. They are chosen from external sources or sometimes from within the pool.

In the following four tables I identified roughly 200 different roles, ordered alphabetically by their departments. Additionally, the tables show my assumptions with regard to the priority (1 means most likely, 3 least likely) for choosing the specific role from studio resources (S), from the pool (P) or from the external market (E).

Sector	Actor	Department	S	P	E
Business	Production Accountant	Accounting	1	2	3
Business	Production Controller	Accounting	1	2	3
Business	Payroll Accountant	Accounting	1	2	3
Business	Asst. Accountant	Accounting	1	2	3
Business	Production Buyer	Accounting	1	2	3
Business	Asst. Production Accountant	Accounting	1	2	3
Business	Construction Accountant	Accounting	1	2	3
Business	Set Cost Accountant	Accounting	1	2	3
Technical	Teacher	Additional Personal	2	1	3
Technical	Safety Coordinator	Additional Personal	2	1	3
Technical	Fire Safety	Additional Personal	2	3	1
Technical	Nurse	Additional Personal	3	1	2
Creative	Set Designer	Art Department / Set Building	2	1	3
Creative	Art Department Coordinator	Art Department / Set Building	2	1	3
Creative	Construction Coordinator Foreman	Art Department / Set Building	1	2	3
Creative	Head Paint Foreman	Art Department / Set Building	1	2	3
Creative	Paint Foreman	Art Department / Set Building	1	2	3
Creative	Stand-by Painter	Art Department / Set Building	1	2	3
Business	Assurance	Assurance	3	1	2
Creative	Casting Director	Cast	2	1	3
Creative	Casting Associate	Cast	2	1	3
Creative	Casting Asst.	Cast	2	1	3
Creative	Talent Agency	Cast	3	1	2
Creative	Extras Casting	Cast	2	1	3
Creative	Actors	Cast	3	1	2
Creative	Stand-Ins	Cast	3	1	2
Creative	Extras	Cast	3	2	1
Creative	Stuntmen	Cast	3	1	2
Creative	Children	Cast	3	1	2
Creative	Animals	Cast	3	1	2
Creative	Animal Trainers	Cast	3	1	2
Technical	Head Caterer	Catering	2	1	3
Creative	Digital Artists	CGI / Composition	2	1	3
Creative	3D Matchmove Artist	CGI / Composition	2	1	3
Creative	CG Artists	CGI / Composition	2	1	3
Creative	Character Animators	CGI / Composition	2	1	3
Creative	Lead Composition Graphics Supervisor	CGI / Composition	2	1	3
Creative	Digital Effects Artists	CGI / Composition	2	1	3
Creative	Digital Matte Artist	CGI / Composition	2	1	3
Creative	Motion Capture Group	CGI / Composition	2	1	3
Creative	Digital Model Development and Construction Artist	CGI / Composition	2	1	3
Creative	Paint Artist	CGI / Composition	2	1	3
Creative	Plate Photography Camera Asst.	CGI / Composition	2	1	3
Creative	Plate Producer	CGI / Composition	2	1	3
Creative	Digital Rotoscope	CGI / Composition	2	1	3
Creative	Director of Photography	Cinematography	2	1	3
Creative	Camera Operators	Cinematography	2	1	3
Creative	Asst. Camera Operators	Cinematography	2	1	3
Creative	Focus Puller	Cinematography	2	1	3
Creative	Steadicam Operator	Cinematography	2	1	3
Creative	Loader/Clapper	Cinematography	2	1	3

Table 1: Organization of the actors of a movie production network (1 of 4)

Sector	Actor	Department	S	P	E
Creative	Still Photographer	Cinematography	2	1	3
Creative	Cable Operator	Cinematography	2	1	3
Technical	Re-Recording Mixer	Dialogue	1	2	3
Technical	ADR Recordist	Dialogue	1	2	3
Technical	Dialog/ADR Editor	Dialogue	1	2	3
Creative	Director	Director	2	1	3
Creative	1. Asst. Director	Director	2	1	3
Creative	2. Asst. Director	Director	2	1	3
Business	Distributor	Distribution	1	2	3
Business	Cinema	Distribution	3	1	2
Business	Video	Distribution	1	2	3
Business	Pay- and FreeTV	Distribution	1	2	3
Business	Merchandising	Distribution	1	2	3
Technical	Cutter/Editor	Editing	2	1	3
Technical	Avid Asst.	Editing	2	1	3
Technical	Asst. Editor	Editing	2	1	3
Technical	Apprentice Editor	Editing	2	1	3
Technical	Dolly Grip	Grip	1	2	3
Technical	Key Rigging Grip	Grip	1	2	3
Technical	Grips	Grip	1	2	3
Business	Investor	Investor	1	2	3
Business	Bank	Investor	3	1	2
Business	Public Film Funding	Investor	3	1	2
Technical	Chief Lighting Technician	Lights and Electrics	1	2	3
Technical	Asst. CLT	Lights and Electrics	1	2	3
Technical	Rigging Gaffer	Lights and Electrics	1	2	3
Technical	Light Technician	Lights and Electrics	1	2	3
Technical	Key Grip	Lights and Electrics	1	2	3
Technical	Best Boy	Lights and Electrics	1	2	3
Technical	Electricians	Lights and Electrics	1	2	3
Technical	Generator Operator	Lights and Electrics	1	2	3
Creative	Location Manager	Location	2	1	3
Creative	Location Scout	Location	2	1	3
Creative	Make Up Supervisor	Make Up and Hair	2	1	3
Creative	Asst. Make Up Supervisor	Make Up and Hair	2	1	3
Creative	Hair Supervisor	Make Up and Hair	2	1	3
Creative	Asst. Hair Supervisor	Make Up and Hair	2	1	3
Creative	Body Make Up	Make Up and Hair	2	1	3
Creative	Stand By	Make Up and Hair	2	1	3
Technical	Copy	Mastering	2	1	3
Technical	Color Timer	Mastering	2	1	3
Technical	Model Supervisor	Miniatures and Models	2	1	3
Technical	Miniature Construction and Photography	Miniatures and Models	2	1	3
Technical	Model Maker	Miniatures and Models	2	1	3
Technical	Orchestrations	Music	2	1	3
Technical	Music Editor	Music	1	2	3
Technical	Asst. Music Editor	Music	1	2	3
Technical	Scoring Engineer	Music	2	1	3
Technical	Scoring Asst.	Music	2	1	3
Technical	Music Preparation	Music	2	1	3

Table 2: Organization of the actors of a movie production network (2 of 4)

Sector	Actor	Department	S	P	E
Technical	Orchestra Leader	Music	2	1	3
Technical	Choir	Music	2	1	3
Technical	Composer	Music	2	1	3
Business	Sequence Supervisor and Development Lead	Post Management	2	1	3
Business	General Management	Post Management	2	1	3
Business	Executive in Charge of Production	Post Management	2	1	3
Business	Post Production Coordinator/Supervisor	Post Management	2	1	3
Business	Visual Effects Coordinator	Post Management	2	1	3
Technical	Visual Effects Production and Technical Support	Post Operations	2	1	3
Technical	Digital Operations and Technology Group	Post Operations	2	1	3
Technical	Machine Room Operators	Post Operations	2	1	3
Technical	Digital Audio Transfer Supervisor	Post Operations	2	1	3
Technical	Video Services	Post Operations	2	1	3
Technical	Projectionist	Post Operations	2	1	3
Technical	Production Network Engineer	Post Operations	2	1	3
Technical	Pre-Visualization Artist	Previsualization and Video Assist	2	1	3
Technical	Video Playback	Previsualization and Video Assist	2	1	3
Technical	Video Assist	Previsualization and Video Assist	2	1	3
Technical	Video Engineer	Previsualization and Video Assist	2	1	3
Technical	Additional Video Asst.	Previsualization and Video Assist	2	1	3
Technical	FX Video Engineer	Previsualization and Video Assist	2	1	3
Technical	Animatronic Model Designer	Previsualization and Video Assist	2	1	3
Technical	3d Modeler	Previsualization and Video Assist	2	1	3
Creative	Art Director	Production Design	2	1	3
Creative	Asst. Art Director	Production Design	2	1	3
Creative	Production Designer	Production Design	2	1	3
Creative	Storyboard Artists	Production Design	2	1	3
Creative	Concept Artist	Production Design	2	1	3
Creative	Chief Sculptor	Production Design	2	1	3
Business	Producer	Production Office	1	2	3
Business	Co Producer	Production Office	2	1	3
Business	Unit Production Manager	Production Office	1	2	3
Business	Production Supervisor/Manager	Production Office	1	2	3
Business	Line Producer	Production Office	1	2	3
Business	Production Coordinator	Production Office	1	2	3
Business	Production Office Coordinator	Production Office	1	2	3
Business	Production Secretary	Production Office	1	2	3
Business	Production Asst.	Production Office	3	2	1
Technical	Painter	Production Services	1	2	3
Technical	Production Services	Production Services	1	2	3
Technical	Tool Foreman	Production Services	1	2	3
Technical	Plaster	Production Services	1	2	3
Technical	Head Greensman	Production Services	1	2	3
Technical	Craft Services	Production Services	1	2	3
Creative	Property Master	Property	2	1	3
Creative	Prop Storeman	Property	1	2	3
Creative	Dressing Propman	Property	2	1	3
Creative	Stand-by	Property	2	1	3
Creative	Set Dressing Coordinator	Property	2	1	3
Creative	Set Decorator	Property	2	1	3

Table 3: Organization of the actors of a movie production network (3 of 4)

Sector	Actor	Department	S	P	E
Technical	Scanning Supervisor	Recording	2	1	3
Technical	Optical Supervisor	Recording	2	1	3
Technical	Film Scanning and Recording	Recording	2	1	3
Creative	Writer	Script	1	2	3
Creative	Literary Agent	Script		2	1
Creative	Author	Script	3	2	1
Creative	Script Supervisor	Script	1	2	3
Technical	Supervisor of Software and Digital Technology	Software	2	1	3
Technical	CG Software Development	Software	2	1	3
Technical	Software Development	Software	2	1	3
Technical	Post Production Sound Services	Sound	1	2	3
Technical	Supervising Sound Editor	Sound	1	2	3
Technical	Asst. Sound Editor	Sound	1	2	3
Technical	Mix Technician	Sound	1	2	3
Technical	Sound Effects Editor	Sound	1	2	3
Technical	Foley Artist	Sound	1	2	3
Technical	Foley Recordist	Sound	1	2	3
Technical	Foley Mixer	Sound	1	2	3
Technical	Foley Editor	Sound	1	2	3
Technical	Cable Operator	Sound	1	2	3
Technical	Sound Editor	Sound	2	1	3
Technical	Sound Mixer	Sound	2	1	3
Technical	Sound Recordist	Sound	2	1	3
Technical	Boom Operator	Sound	2	1	3
Technical	Sound Asst.	Sound	2	1	3
Technical	SFX Pyrotechnics	Special FX	2	1	3
Technical	Special FX Foreman	Special FX	2	1	3
Technical	SFX Engineer	Special FX	2	1	3
Technical	SFX Rigging	Special FX	2	1	3
Technical	FX Supervisor	Special FX	2	1	3
Technical	FX Artist	Special FX	2	1	3
Business	Studio Executive	Studio	1		
Business	Creative Production	Studio	1	2	3
Business	Business Affairs	Studio	1	2	3
Business	Legal Affairs	Studio	1	2	3
Technical	Transportation	Transport	2	1	3
Technical	Drivers	Transport	2	1	3
Technical	Helicopters	Transport	2	1	3
Creative	VFX Producer	Visual FX	2	1	3
Creative	VFX Art Director	Visual FX	2	1	3
Creative	VFX Coordinator	Visual FX	2	1	3
Creative	Co Visual FX Supervisor	Visual FX	2	1	3
Creative	VFX Editor	Visual FX	2	1	3
Creative	Conceptual Artist	Visual FX	2	1	3
Creative	Visual Effects Storyboard	Visual FX	2	1	3
Creative	Costume Designer	Wardrobe	2	1	3
Creative	Costume Supervisor	Wardrobe	2	1	3
Creative	Costumers	Wardrobe	2	1	3
Creative	Textile Arts	Wardrobe	1	2	3

Table 4: Organization of the actors of a movie production network (4 of 4)

The following class diagram shows an overview of a production network. The departments are modeled as classes and the roles within the departments are modeled as attributes. The positions of the classes correspond to the structure built up in Figure 37.

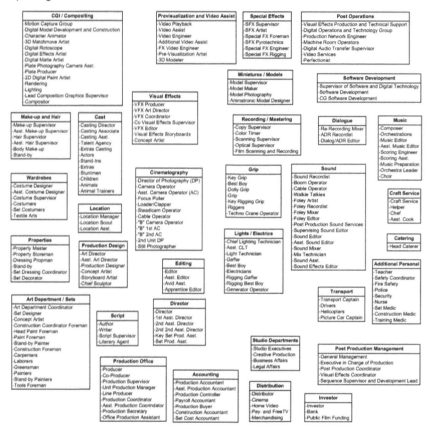

Figure 38: Organizational overview of the production departments

5.2 Data Architecture: Content and Artifacts

In the following paragraph the movie as a product is structured itself. During the production process, various departments implement small elements which are later on composited into the final movie or into related products. These elements are designated as technical artifacts. In addition, management artifacts are created to support the production process. The interdependencies between managerial and technical artifacts throughout almost every step of the production process support the requirement for an integrated platform.

The constitutive elements of a movie are classified in Figure 39.

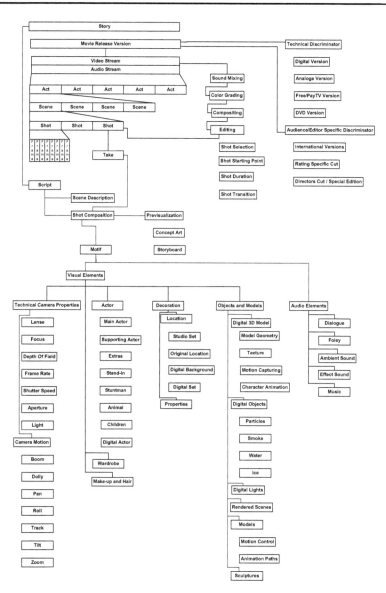

Figure 39: Structure of digital elements of a movie

In general, a movie is an audio-visual translation of a story. The basic – and throughout the entire production process underlying – artifact is the script or screenplay. It describes the storyline, the screen actors, their dialogue and action in a specific time and environment. The script is divided into specific acts and scenes. For each scene the syntax and semantics of the involved visual and audio elements are described in the script. The director and the director of photography work closely together on a shot decomposition for the individual scenes, dividing each scene into motifs, camera angles and intercuts. Several takes are filmed from each shot. And finally, each shot is a sequence of single frames. Consequently, the elementary artifacts comprising a movie are sequences of pictures and audio files.[161]

Visual elements are concretized in the shot decomposition, which gives information on the action executed by the different types of screen actors shown on picture. It also describes their attributes like wardrobe, hair and make-up. Also, information about weather, time of day and decoration in which the action takes place is defined, e.g. a studio set or an original set, as well as the necessary properties or miniatures and models to equip the set. This information is taken from the script and collected on breakdown sheets. Furthermore, the director of photography specifies how to shoot a scene in advance by defining the technical attributes of the camera, for example the choice of lenses, depth of field, light, or camera motion in relation to the action in frame. The camera report lists in detail the settings actually applied during the shot. Most any visual element in a frame can be a digital element. The director must therefore decide, in collaboration with his visual effects consultants, which elements are to be created digitally (i.e. separately) for compositing to the final frame during post-production. The digital elements can be three-dimensional models as well as two-dimensional artwork, either static or dynamic. They may cover animated characters, static models, 2D background plates or a diversity of environmental elements like smoke, fog, water, snow, etc.

The audio elements of a scene consist of dialogue, ambient sound, foley sound, sound effects and, of course, the music. Every element is generated separately, and at the end of post-production their ratio is mixed carefully to achieve the desired expression.

---

[161] See Faulstich (2000), p. 201.

The actual release versions of the movie are created in post-production. A movie consists of scenes that are composited from numerous visual elements. These scenes are edited, meaning that they are augmented with starting points, durations and transitions. The different scenes are mastered to achieve a continuous and homogenous image quality by color grading and other process steps. Finally, the audio elements are mixed and aligned to the scenes.

In the end, it is not just a single movie that is produced. Depending on the audience and the technical preconditions of the presentation device, different products are assembled during post-production.

The last paragraph enumerated the content information generated during the individual production steps, as well as the descriptive meta-data information assigned to each element. Much of this meta-data information is collected by hand or in heterogeneous systems, and is either not accessible in following production steps or has to be extracted manually with extra effort. Examples are shooting instructions stemming from a shot decomposition during pre-production, executed on set by the camera operators and logged manually on a camera report during production. The editor ultimately aligns these to the digital shots to organize his files during post-production. I argue that an integrated production system supporting a standardized description language for the content produced would allow for fundamental improvements during production and utilization of audio-visual content.

The proposed reference model is based on a continuous description of each content element using the standardized MPEG-7 description language. Figure 40 below shows the structure of the digital element description.[162] All descriptive information mentioned above, whether syntactic or semantic, can be modeled as MPEG-7 meta-data.

---

[162] See also Chapter 2.3.

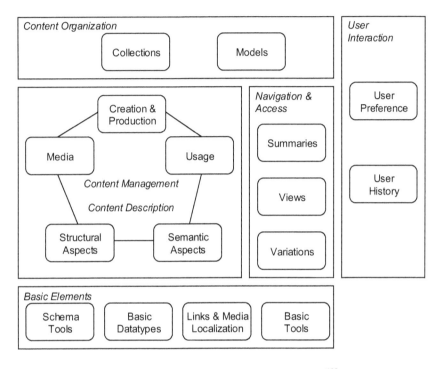

Figure 40: MPEG-7 digital elements structure[163]

---

[163] Based on Pereira/Koenen (2001) p. 543.

5.3 Application Architecture: Use Case Overview

In the following tables, the information gathered in the case study and modeled into use cases describing the main actors and their responsibilities during the different phases of the production process are condensed to extract the diverse applications in each process step. I present one table for each process phase (development, packaging, pre-production, production, and post-production) in the meta-model structure described in Chapter 3.2 and Chapter 4.3. I assign the determined use cases to the different production processes (business modeling and requirements, analysis and design, implementation and test, and deployment) and to the supporting processes (project management, organizational environment, and technical infrastructure). For each use case I identify the basic technical and managerial artifacts and the most common tools used in the industry. In addition, for each use case I present the influence of the ongoing digitization in the entire movie production process. I give an overview of the implications of a use case to other areas and their integration potential as a result. While analyzing and clustering the use cases I discovered six essential functional components, into which I subsume every use case. The components I defined are input factor market, scripting, budgeting, scheduling, media asset management and communications, and financing and payment. In these tables I reduced the number of discovered use cases from 177 to 94 essential use cases which can be supported by an integrated production system.

	No	Production of the Prototyp Development / Idea — Use Case	Components	Artifacts	Tools	Digitization	Implications/Integration
Business Modeling	1	Aquire rights to story	MPC	Contract	Market Place (MP), Contract	Digital Contracts, MP	faster, broader Overview
	2	Develop script	SCR	Script	Movie Magic (MM), Scripting	Digital Script	Integration Budet / Schedule
Requirements							
Analysis	4	Prepare preliminary budget	BUD	Budget	MM Budgeting		Integration Scripting / Schedule
Design							
Implementation							
Test							
Deployment							
Project Management	5	Schedule and supervise the development activities	SCH / SCH	Schedule	MS Project / MM Scheduling		Integration Scripting / Schedule
Organizational Environment	6	Select and hire writer	MPC	Contract	MP, Pool, Database	Digital Contracts, MP	
	7	Select and hire director	MPC	Contract	MP, Pool, Database	Digital Contracts, MP	
	8	Select and hire line producer	MPC	Contract	MP, Pool, Database	Digital Contracts, MP	
Technical Infrastructure							

Production Processes (Business Modeling through Deployment)
Supporting Processes (Project Management through Technical Infrastructure)

MPC | Input Factor Market Place and Contracts
SCR | Scripting
BUD | Budgeting
SCH | Scheduling
MAM | MAM and Communications
FIN | Financing and Payment

Table 5: Use cases in the development phase, digital artifacts and tools

The development phase, described in Table 5 is characterized by the initial combination of creative input factors. In addition to the content - the rights to a story – the producer hires the basic creative actors. The involved functional component is the input factor market, offering the service to find, negotiate, handle, control, and adjust transactions of property rights, thereby reducing transaction costs. The resulting managerial and technical artifacts are the contracts between the actors. In the development phase a preliminary script based upon the acquired rights to a story must be developed. The functional component involved is the scripting component. A common tool is a scripting tool like "Movie Magic Scripting", distributed by Entertainment Partners.[164] The resulting technical artifact is, of course, the preliminary script. A close interconnection exists between the continuously modified script and the preliminary budget and schedule set up during the development phase. The scheduling task is executed within the project management and scheduling component. A widely used tool is "Movie Magic Scheduling". It supports the breakdown process of an imported script by analyzing and enumerating the designed elements, provided they are tagged properly with meta-information like „Actor", "property", or "environmental specification". The resulting managerial artifact is the schedule. The schedule can in turn be imported into the budgeting component, designing a budget based upon the desired elements listed in the breakdown sheet and the developed shooting schedule. Application of the tool "Movie Magic Budgeting" is widespread within the industry. The interconnections between the different functional components and the constant exchange of artifacts call for artifact storage in a common asset management system. In my model, this is organized in the media asset management and communications component.

---

[164] For further information on the Movie Magic products see Entertainment Partners (2005).

Production of the Prototyp
Packaging (Bundling, Distri, Financing)

	No	Use Case	Components	Artifacts	Tools	Digitization	Implications/Integration
Business Modeling							
Requirements	10	Contract stars and talents	MPC, SCH	Contract	MP, Prod, Database	Digital Contracts / MP	Integration DBs / Schedule
	11	Request team members	MPC	Contract	MP, Prod, Database	Digital Contracts / MP	Integration DBs / Schedule
	12	Check crew availabilities	MPC	Contract	MP, Prod, Database	Digital Contracts / MP	Integration DBs / Schedule
	13	Select and hire production supervisor	MPC	Contract	MP, Prod, Database	Digital Contracts / MP	Integration DBs / Schedule
	14	Select and hire visual effects companies	FIN, MAM	Contract	MP, Prod, Database	Digital Contracts / MP	Integration DBs / Schedule
	30	Secure all clearances and releases	BUD	Cash Flow Chart	eg SPoints Administration Tool	Digital Contracts / MP	Easier to administrate
	33	Prepare a cash flow chart	FIN	Cash Flow Chart			Integration Budget
	34	Prepare recoupment plan	MPC	Contract	MP, Prod, Database	Digital Contracts / MP	Integration Budget
	35	Find investors					
Analysis	16	Refine schedule and budget	BUD, SCH	Schedule / Budget	MM Budgeting / Scheduling	Digital Contracts / MP	Integration Budget / Schedule
Design	17	Refine script	SCR	Script	MM Scripting		
	18	Get bids on equipment	MPC	Contract	MP, Prod, Database		Integration Scripting
Implementation	19	Submit script to research company	MAM				
Test							
Deployment							
Project Management							
Organizational Environment							
Technical Infrastructure							

Production Processes · *Supporting Processes*

MPC Input Factor Market Place and Contracts
SCR Scripting
BUD Budgeting
SCH Scheduling
MAM MAM and Communications
FIN Financing and Payment

Table 6: Use cases in the packaging phase, digital artifacts and tools

The packaging phase is specified in Table 6. In this phase the script, schedule and budget are worked out in a concerted way. Their artifacts, components and interconnections have already been discussed above. The production network of management, artists, distributors, and investors must also be initialized. Again, the component input factor market supports this process with a service platform for these particular transactions. The resulting managerial artifacts are contracts between the involved actors. The Studio System applies the basic approach to supporting the transactions' information phase by managing the pool of industry members. It is a comprehensive and frequently utilized online database selling up-to-date information on practically every member of the Hollywood industry, including details about their past and ongoing productions, and their contact data. The original developers of the "Movie Magic" product series run The Studio System.[165]

---

[165] For detailed information about The Studio System see Studio System Inc. (2005).

	No	Use Case	Components	Artifacts	Tools	Digitization	Implications/Integration
Business Modeling	39	Production executive meeting	MAM		Video Conferencing		
Requirements	40	Investigate product placement	FIN	Contracts			
Analysis	41	Breakdown and refine script	SCR, BUD, SCH	Schedule/Budget	MM Budgeting / Scheduling		
Design	42	Monitor changing script	SCR, BUD, SCH	Script	MM Scripting, Communication		
	43	Manage script rewrites in time	SCR, BUD, SCH	Script	MM Scripting, Communication		
	44	Distribute scripts and paperwork	SCR, BUD, SCH	Script	MM Scripting, Communication		
	45	Breakdown in extras, stunts, effects etc.	SCR, BUD, SCH	Schedule/Budget	MM Budgeting / Scheduling		
	46	Line-up requirements, green screen, miniatures	SCR, BUD, SCH	Schedule/Budget	MM Budgeting / Scheduling		Integration to Script
	48	Create previsualizations	MAM	Previs Scenes	3D Games Engines, Video		Integration to VFX 3D Models
	49	Create storyboards	MAM	Storyboard	Digital Storyboarder	digital Storyboard	Integration to Script Lines
	51	Find and hold stages	MPC	Contracts	MP. Pool, Database		
	52	Scout locations	MPC	Contracts	Database, Digital Database	Digital Database	Integration Previs
	53	Study past weather	MPC	Database	Digital Database		
	55	Secure locations	MPC	Contracts			
Implementation	56	Prepare cast head shots for doubles and stand-ins	MAM	Foto	Digital Camera, MAM		
Test	57	Arrange still photo sessions	MAM	Foto	Digital Camera, MAM		
Deployment	60	Inform wardrobe of cast info	MAM				
Project Management	64	Define pre-production schedule	SCH	Schedule	MM Scheduling, MS Project		
	65	Create final schedule	SCH	Schedule	MM Scheduling		Integration Budget
	66	Sign-off on final budget	BUD	Budget	MM Budgeting		Integration Schedule
	67	Create day out of days	SCH				
Organizational Environment	72	Hire cast and crew	MPC	Contracts	MP. Pool, Database	Support Pool via E-Community	Integration Schedule
	74	Cast film	MPC	Contracts	MP. Pool, Database	Support Pool via E-Community	Integration Schedule
	76	Prepare cast deals	MPC	Contracts	MP. Pool, Database	Support Pool via E-Community	Integration Schedule
	77	Hire key crew	MPC	Contracts	MP. Pool, Database	Support Pool via E-Community	Integration Budget/Payment
	78	Negotiate crew deals	MPC	Contracts	MP. Pool, Database	Support Pool via E-Community	Integration Budget/Payment
	79	Hire asst. production coordinator and p. asst.	MPC	Contracts	MP. Pool, Database	Support Pool via E-Community	Integration Schedule
	80	Select 1st. asst. director	MPC	Contracts	MP. Pool, Database	Support Pool via E-Community	Integration Schedule
	81	Select script supervisor	MPC	Contracts	MP. Pool, Database	Support Pool via E-Community	Integration Budget/Payment
	84	Accounting procedures to department heads	FIN, BUD	Reports	Payment System		Integration Budget
	86	Handle time cards & payroll	FIN, SCH	Reports	Payment System		Integration Budget
Technical Infrastructure	89	Negotiate equipment deals	MPC, SCH, BUD	Contracts	MP. Pool, Database	Digital Equipment	Integration Budget/Payment
	90	Order film and equipment	MPC, SCH, BUD	Contracts	MP. Pool, Database	Digital Equipment	Integration Budget/Payment
	91	Line-up lab, sound house, dubbing facilities	SCH, MPC, BUD	Contracts	MP. Pool, Database	Digital Equipment	Integration Schedule
	92	Set up editing rooms	SCH, MPC, BUD	Contracts	MP. Pool, Database	Digital Equipment	Integration Schedule

MPC | Input Factor Market Place and Contracts
SCR | Scripting
BUD | Budgeting
SCH | Scheduling
MAM | MAM and Communications
FIN | Financing and Payment

Table 7: Use cases in the pre-production phase, digital artifacts and tools

Table 7 describes the pre-production phase. In this phase script, schedule and budget are again refined, with significant interdependency. Human resources and technical infrastructure have to be selected and their contracts have to be closed via the input factor market component. Some early artistic elements implementing the script, such as storyboards or pre-visualization scenes are developed. Along with the technical artifacts and the script, these elements must be managed in the media asset management and communications component.

Production of the Prototyp Production

	No	Use Case	Components	Artifacts	Tools	Digitization	Implications/Integration
Business Modeling							
Requirements							
Analysis							
Design							
Implementation	94	Cinematography	MAM	Digital Picture, Sound, Information	HD Cam	Digital Film	Integrate Script
	103	Greenscreen compositing	MAM	Digital Picture, Sound, Information	Compositing SW	Filming of foreground Elements	Integrate Script
	105	CGI	MAM	Digital Scene	3D SMAX	Adding and editing Scenes	Integrate Script
	106	Motion capturing and animation	MAM	Digital Scene		Digital Characters	Integrate Script
Test	113	Cut dailies	MAM	Digital Scene	AVID	Editing on set	
	114	Coordinate screening of dailies	MAM	Digital Scene	AVID	Screening at once	
	115	Oversee day-to-day production	MAM	Digital Scene	AVID	Screening at once	
Deployment							
Project Management	118	Check and distribute weather reports	SCH, BUD	Call Sheet	MM Scheduling, Budgeting, Scripting		
	119	Adjust shooting schedules	SCH, BUD	Schedule	MM Scheduling		
	120	Issue work calls	SCH, BUD	Call Sheet	MM Scheduling		
	121	Order standries and extras	MPC, BUD	Contract	MF Pool, Database		
	122	Prepare call sheets for cast and crew	SCH, BUD	Call Sheet	MM Scheduling		
	124	Monitor script changes	SCR, BUD	Script	MM Scripting, Budgeting, Scheduling		
	125	Prepare call sheets & production reports	SCH, BUD	Call Sheet/Production Reports	MM Scheduling, Budgeting, Scripting		
	126	Submit daily/weekly production reports	SCH, BUD		MM Scheduling, Budgeting, Scripting		
	127	Prepare daily & weekly cost reports	BUD		MM Budgeting, Payment		
	128	Monitor schedule and budget	SCH, BUD		MM Scheduling, Budgeting, Scripting		
	129	Control cash flow	BUD, SCH		MM Budgeting, Payment		
	131	Coordinate delivery of film to the lab	MAM	Digital Scene			
Organizational Environment	139	Submit workers compensation claim forms	FIN				
Technical Infrastructure							

Legend:

MPC Input Factor Market Place and Contracts
SCR Scripting
BUD Budgeting
SCH Scheduling
MAM MAM and Communications
FIN Financing and Payment

Table 8: Use cases in the production phase, digital artifacts and tools

In the production phase described in Table 8, the digital content elements are developed during creative tasks. These elements must initially be imported into the system, for example from a digital camera, and managed in the media asset management and communications component. Most transformations on these elements require specialized external software products like the de-facto industry standard in non-linear video editing solutions, the Avid Media Composer, often simply described as Avid, or the audio production standard, Pro Tools HD by Digidesign, also a division of Avid.[166] During the production phase these technical artifacts are repeatedly included and excluded. As mentioned above, some meta-information about the content of the created artifacts has already been described during the scripting and breakdown steps. There is essential integration potential for the elements managed in the media asset management and communications component and the scripting component. Technical artifacts in the scheduling and budgeting component, like call sheets and production reports, can also be integrated into the meta-information of the created content. Additionally, technical information gathered during the creation or transformation action steps describe the digital elements in even more detail. During the production phase the script, schedule and budget change, triggered by a variety of conditions. This will certainly influence the financial management component.

---

[166] For more information on editing software solutions see Avid (2005) and Digidesign (2005).

	No	Use Case (Production of the Prototyp / Production (Post-production))	Components	Artifacts	Tools	Digitization	Implications/Integration
Business Modeling							
Requirements							
Analysis							
Design							
Implementation							
Test	151	View and analyze directors rough cut	MAM	Rough Cut	AVD		
	152	Prepare additional photography	SCH BUD	Schedule, Budget	MM Scheduling, Budget, Scripting multiple Tools		
	153	Supervise visual effects	MAM	SFX Scenes	Pro Tools		
	154	Supervise automated dialog replacement	MAM	ADR Sound	AVD		
	155	Edit the film	MAM	Cutted Movie	Pro Tools		
	156	Create and mix the sound design	MAM	Sound	Pro Tools		
	157	Score the music	MAM	Music	Pro Tools		
	158	Create the final dub	MAM	Release Version and Single Elements			
Deployment	161	Turn over files, inventory of company assets, log of insurance claims & notes	MAM	Release Version			
	162	Fulfill studio delivery requirements and turn-over elements	MAM				
	163	Schedule release dates and distribution philosophy	SCH	Marketing Plan			
	164	Sell foreign rights, cable, TV, etc.	FIN	Contract	eg 3Points Administration Tool AVD	Digital Contract	
	165	Cut trailers	MAM	Trailer			
	166	Design poster and press kit	SCH	Marketing Material			
	167	Schedule press junkets	SCH	Marketing Plan			
	169	Release the film	MAM				
Project Management	173	Oversee post-production activities	SCH BUD	Scheduling	MS Project		
	174	Issue post-production schedule					
Organizational Environment	176	Examine final bills	FIN BUD	Reports	Payment		Easier to administrate
Technical Infrastructure							

Production Processes — Supporting Processes

MFC Input Factor Market Place and Contracts
SCR Scripting
BUD Budgeting
SCH Scheduling
MAM MAM and Communications
FIN Financing and Payment

Table 9: Use cases in the post-production phase, digital artifacts and tools

The post-production phase as described in Table 9: Use cases in the post-production phase, digital artifacts and tools involve components similar to the ones described in the production phase for transforming the technical artifacts. The media asset management and communications component plays the leading role in importing and exporting files as well as in adjusting their meta-information by integrating all relevant descriptions associated with each particular element.

Table 10: Connection between use cases, roles and artifacts[167]

Legend:

DEV	Development / Idea
PAC	Packaging / Bundling, Distr., Finance
PRE	Pre-production
PRO	Production
POS	Post-production

MPC	Input Factor Market Place and Contracts
SCR	Scripting
BUD	Budgeting
SCH	Scheduling
MAM	MAM and Communications
FIN	Financing and Payment

A	accumulate
M	modify
R	read
D	delete
X	execute

---

[167] This table serves as overview, please see Appendix 1 to 4 (pp. 145-148) for an enlarged version

Table 10 gives a complete overview of every analyzed use case in each production phase, subdivided into the different production and supporting processes. The basic component involved in each use case is represented. The executing actors (X) of each use case are described and classified in their respective departments. Finally, the technical and managerial artifacts are listed, in combination with information on whether the artifact has been applied (A), modified (M) or read (R) by an actor during this use case.

5.4 Technical Architecture: Components and Services

In prior paragraphs the actors and departments were modeled and their assigned use cases were specified. I sorted the use cases to corresponding components by function. These functional components are implemented in a variety of specialized software solutions. The results of each production step performed on such a component can be described as technical or managerial artifacts. In addition to the technical artifacts, the managerial artifacts also contain important information to completely describe the digital content elements using the MPEG-7 meta-description language. This content processing is necessary to support efficient management of the increasing volume of digital information produced during movie productions, as well as the diversity of exploitation possibilities of this content. A common description language is important in the attempt to support integration of isolated components. I analyzed their integration potential above.

The system I model is based on the perspective of the producer. He is the orchestrator of the production network. He has to assemble the participating actors, determine the business process, supervise the efforts of all departments and secure the production of his assets. For this he must quickly and reliably integrate the different IT systems used by all of his important business partners. Considering a major Hollywood production company, some 20 project networks must be set up from scratch every year, integrating into each a variety of partners with heterogeneous IT systems that are constantly being replaced to keep up with the fast pace of development.

As described in Chapter 3, these requirements demand an IT architecture in line with the Service Oriented Architecture (SOA) . The different layers of SOA are, from top to bottom: the graphical user interface (GUI), the choreography layer supporting the business process logic, the composition layer automating the processes and addressing web services, the core web services offering interfaces to the component layer and finally the data layer.

With SOA the producer gets an IT infrastructure that supports production activities on the business process level. These are modeled by activity diagrams using the Unified Modeling Language 2 (UML2) that can, in turn, be translated into the Business Process Execution Language (BPEL). The business process management server that orchestrates the collaboration between diverse partners understands the processes modeled in BPEL. The IT systems of these partners are encapsulated into functional components that can be accessed via a web service interfaces. In the following, I describe the static structure of the components before I model the dynamic behavior of the business processes in the following Chapter.

The architecture model is made up of ten components. The top layer of the model is the graphical user interface. The central business process management server is situated on the choreography and composition layer. I modeled interfaces between the different functional components and the business process management server on the core web service layer. The component layer comprises the functional component scripting, project management and scheduling, budgeting, financial management, input factor markets, media asset management and communications. The data layer holds only the various databases accessed in conjunction with the media asset management and communications component. The interfaces to external content creation and modification devices are modeled as black boxes. Their internal events are not included in this model, albeit they are accessed frequently during the production process.

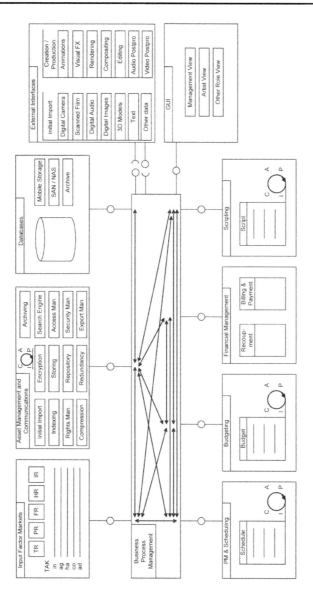

Figure 41: Reference architecture model

Business Process Management:

The core of my architecture model is the business process management server that integrates the different components using a bus topology. All business logic is defined and executed on this server. Later on I will model the dynamic workflows in detail. Basic qualities of these workflows are the collaboration of different components. In the architecture model arrows represent the interdependencies between components. They can be read as follows:

Modifications to the script obviously have an impact on the schedule and the budget. Script modifications can also impact the input factor market if, for example, these include changes in locations or screen actors. Finally, the script as digital content is managed and stored via the media asset management and communications component.

Modifications to the budget may demand adaptations to the script and the corresponding schedule. Also it predetermines negotiations with different resources from the input factor markets. The budget, which is stored by the media asset management and communications component, is closely interconnected with the financial management.

Modifications to the schedule influence both the script and the budget. When the schedule is changed, it often affects the financial management. In most cases the input factor market is accessed to reconfigure the contracts with specific resources. As with the budget and the script, the schedule is stored by the media asset management and communications component.

Modifications to the financial management are fundamentally interconnected with the budget and the schedule. Financial management information is aligned with the corresponding content elements via the media asset management and communications component.

Modifications to the input factor market impact the script, the schedule and the budget. The negotiated contracts are stored and aligned with the content elements within the media asset management and communications component.

The media asset management and communications component has direct access to the databases.

Scripting:

The scripting component is responsible for the creation and modification of the screenplay. As I mentioned above, the script is the fundamental description of every content element to be produced. Using the interface to the scripting component, attributes from the script must be aligned with content elements, schedule information, budget information and resource information. The actions within the scripting component are iterative, underlying a classic control loop with four phases: analysis (A), planning (P), implementation (I), and control (C). The subsequent adoption phase is actually the analysis phase of the next iteration. The tool used within the scripting component is a specialized word processor like "Movie Magic Scripting".

Project Management and Scheduling:

The project management and scheduling component is responsible for the generation and supervision of a working plan for the movie production. In this component, requirements set forth by the script and the input factor market must be transformed into a realizable schedule. The schedule must be updated regularly. As such, the project management and scheduling actions are iterative and underlie the aforementioned control loop. The tool used within the project management and scheduling component is a specialized planning tool like "Movie Magic Scheduling".

Budgeting:

The budgeting component generates the budget based on the script and the associate schedule. The budget is adapted throughout the production process in accordance with changes in the script, the schedule or in the input factor market. The budget is, of course, also influenced and limited by the available investment capital managed in the financial management component. Here again, budgeting underlies the iterative steps of the control loop. The tool used within the budgeting component is a specialized budgeting tool like "Movie Magic Budgeting".

Financial Management:

The financial management component is divided into two elements, the billing and payment element and the recoupment element. In the billing and payment element the day-to-day cash flow is handled, whereas in the recoupment element investments and predicted revenues by exploiting the distribution rights are managed. Via the interface the financial management component is certainly interconnected with the budget component. But moreover the distribution rights for each content element have to be determined. The financial management component uses accounting software.

Input Factor Market:

The input factor market component is a complex module supporting resource transactions. I divided the resources into technical, physical, financial, human, and intangible resources. For each resource, specific marketplaces that can be integrated into the production system either already exist or are in development. Integrated marketplaces reduce transaction costs by supporting the initiation, agreement, handling, control, and adjustment phase of the transaction. Technical resources are the technical equipment required for shooting the movie, e.g. lights or cameras. They can be obtained on the marketplace for technical equipment. Physical resources are buildings or working capital. Specialized databases list stages and locations for hire that fulfill specific requirements for a given movie production. Financial resources are equity capital or bank financing. Investors and distributors available for project support can be found on film marketplaces. Human resources are both creative personnel and network contacts to partnering companies. In addition to marketplaces for screen actors, there are specialized marketplaces for practically every other kind of crew required for a movie production. Intangible resources are, for example, rights to material. Story rights and script can be obtained on literary marketplaces. Most current solutions for resource acquisition are limited to the initiation phase in which detailed information about a particular partner can be gathered. By integrating the contracting process and payment and after-sales service into the solution, the agreement and handling phases can be supported, thereby reducing overall transaction costs. There are extensive interconnections between the information and contracts gathered in the input factor market component and the budgeting, scripting and scheduling component. Tools for input factor markets are, e.g. industry databases like The Studio System which, however provide only the raw data.

Media Asset Management and Communications:

The media asset management and communications component manages the digital content produced and accesses the databases. Individual elements are developed in iterations. An iteration comprises the control flow steps of analysis, planning, implementation and control. The following crucial sub-components of this component describe how a single content element is handled within the whole production system. A digital content element from outside the production system is imported via external interfaces. Next the element is indexed, either manually or automatically. Technical meta-information from the external interfaces is aligned with the content using the MPEG-7 description language. Descriptive meta-information from other components, and of course manual indices from an actor are stored in the MPEG-7 description. Then access and use rights are defined and managed. The digital element is compressed using an adequately fast and non-lossy algorithm. The production system enables collaborative work over the internet. To secure the transmission of data, content must be encrypted efficiently. The digital element is then stored in the databases. During the production process, it is important that content elements are accessed via a repository that handles concurrent use and keeps a version history of the elements. Digital elements are very valuable – a loss of data could mean a financial loss on the scale of the entire production budget. As such, redundant content storage is crucial. Following the production phase, digital elements that no longer need to be accessed regularly can be archived, on tape for example. MPEG-7 descriptors offer a powerful way to specify content elements, thereby making quick access to specific digital content files possible. A search engine within the media asset management and communications component finds elements corresponding to the search query. The access management sub-component decides whether the requesting actor or component is certified and has sufficient rights to access the element in question. The security management sub-component ensures the secure, encrypted transmission of data between the database and the requesting partner. Elements are watermarked robustly and invisibly with information about the transaction allowing this information to be reconstructed in the case of rights violation. The information embedded in the watermark is impervious to significant amounts further editing. Ultimately, the export management sub-component delivers the content element to the intended recipient. Specialized software solutions exist for every media asset management and communications sub-component.

Databases:

Databases store the digital elements during movie production. Depending on the desired scenario, different types of databases make sense. Digital cameras demand mobile storage solutions. They are usually small in size and just fast enough to write the incoming data rate. After the initial import of the elements into the production system, many users need to access files quickly and concurrently.

For this, high performance storage systems like storage area networks (SAN) or network attached storage (NAS) systems consisting of RAID disk arrays are necessary. Finally, the produced digital elements have to be archived to free the disk arrays for the next project.

External Interfaces:

The external interfaces are modeled as interfaces for handling requests to and from the production system. There is not a single interface as there is between the business process management server and the other components. Instead there are many, one for each sub-component of the external interface component. This component can be divided into "initial import" elements and "creation and production" elements. I subsume digital film from cameras, analog film scanned to digital, digital audio elements, digital images, 3D models, text and other raw material under initial import. These digital elements are imported once via the interface. There are also numerous external software components for handling creative and productive processing steps like animation, visual effects, rendering, compositing, editing, audio post-production, and video post-production. They access the digital elements for their processing steps via the media asset management and communications component. Each step affects the MPEG-7 descriptions of the element. They must be modified both automatically with information from within the processing history and other technical specifications, and manually by the artist.

Graphical User Interface:

The graphical user interface, which is not included in my reference model, offers a variety of views of the production process. For example, the managerial view shows the production process and effort to the executives.

5.5 Information Architecture: Processes

The dynamic behavior of the production system is modeled in the following paragraph. The producer as orchestrator of the production network designs and controls the collaborative business processes. The business process management server hosts the business logic and executes the action sequences that are strongly distributed among diverse components. The components are accessed as encapsulated web services.

I model the business processes using UML2 activity diagrams. They can be easily translated into BPEL (Business Process Execution Language) , which can be read and executed by an integration server.

As mentioned in earlier paragraphs, many actions follow a control loop. These loops are modeled in advance and are utilized in later models. Although they are similar to each other, I divide the loops into two categories, a transaction loop and a creation loop. Each loop consists of five actions, whereas the last action step, the adjustment action, closes the circle and starts a new iteration of the loop at the first action step.

The transaction loop shown in Figure 42 is generated by the often-discovered use case "select and hire". Based on the need to add a certain entity to the production network and on defined requirements for one of the five resource categories, technical resources, physical resources, financial resources, human resources, or intangible resources, the control loop starts with the first action step, the gathering of information. In the next step, agreement between the partners is negotiated. In the third step, the actual transaction is handled and the property rights are transferred. In the fourth step the transaction is checked and eventually adjusted within the fifth step.

The creation loop extracted from the use case "create and revise" shown in Figure 43 works similarly. A digital content element has to be created. Certain requirements are defined for this element. In the first action step these requirements are analyzed. Possibilities for implementing the element in accordance with the requirements are planned within the second action step. In the third action step the element is actually designed. A control step at position four resolves whether this element can be finalized or whether it has to be adjusted in step five. Then the next iteration occurs and the creation loop starts over again based upon the adjusted requirements and the preliminary digital content element.

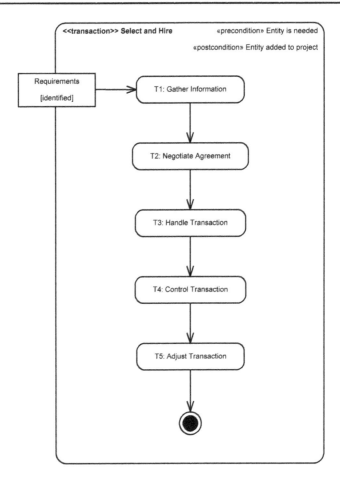

Figure 42: Reference process: Select and Hire

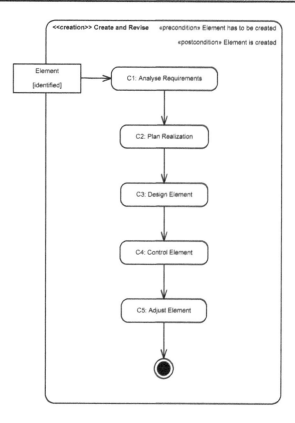

Figure 43: Reference process: Create and Revise

In the following, I model the business processes of a movie production from the perspective of the producer and the business process management server. The processes are divided into the discovered production processes – business modeling and requirement, analysis and design, implementation and test, and deployment – as well as the supporting processes – organizational environment, project management and technical infrastructure.

Even though the UML2 activity diagrams are self-explanatory, I give a brief basic description for each model, in which I specify the goal, the initialization, the addressed web services (the functional components), some significant action steps, the artifacts, the interruptions and signals to other processes.

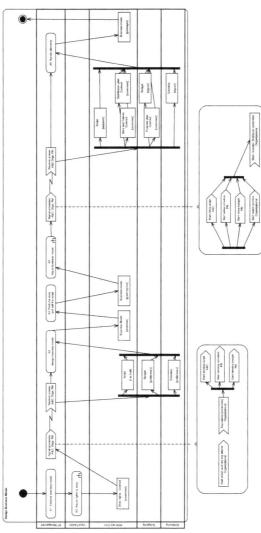

Figure 44: Activity diagram of the production process: Business Modeling and Requirements[168]

---

[168] This table serves as overview, please see Appendix 5 to 7 (pp. 149-151) for an enlarged version

The first activity diagram, shown in Figure 44, models the production process: business modeling and requirements. The goal of this activity is to design a working business model for a product – the movie to be produced. The activity starts with the intention of the producer or the studio to produce a movie and often the action step of buying the rights to a certain story for a specified period of time. A positive result of the business modeling process is a packaged business model on which the pre-production phase of a movie production can be started. Nevertheless, only a small percentage of movie projects in development are actually shot. A negative post-condition is that the story rights fall back to the property owner. During the business modeling and requirements process the business process management server addresses the input factor market component to select and hire key personal, the media asset management and communications component where the script in different stages is stored, as well as the scheduling and budgeting components. As can be seen in the activity diagram, the action „acquire rights to story" is initiated by the business process management server and is executed in the input factor market component. It is a complex action, designated by the fork-symbol, following the reference process "select and hire" discussed above. The bundled business model consists of a script, a schedule, and a budget, as well as contracts with the key personnel, the investors and distributors. The business modeling process is interrupted by phases during the analysis and design process in which the script is written and in the organizational environment process in which key personnel is selected and hired.

The following two activity diagrams, Figure 45 and Figure 46, model the analysis and design process. The goal of the activity is to analyze and design every necessary production artifact with respect to the requirements collected in the business modeling and requirements process. The business process management server starts the process, ordering the development of a script. The process is initiated by a signal from the organizational environment process, with the message that the key talents have committed to the project. At this point the story rights have already been acquired. The business process management server addresses the scripting, budgeting and scheduling components that work closely together during the development of the script, as well as the media asset management and communications component in which the artifacts are stored. Some pre-visualizations to specify the look of the film are created outside of the production system. To this end, external interfaces are accessed. Script development is an iterative process, following the reference process "create and revise". The scripting component, the budgeting component and the scheduling component exchange their progress frequently to adjust and improve their artifacts. A preliminary script, schedule and budget are generated to build up a business model. The process is paused until the business modeling and requirements process sends a signal indicating the business model has been greenlighted. Now the next iteration in refining script, schedule and budget can start. After the business model is packaged, the script elements are broken down to specify the look of the film and to align all requirements for shooting the film. Due to the fact that the script is still in development, some action steps will have to be repeated until the final script, schedule and budget meet the requirements set forth by the business modeling and requirements process. The analysis and design process then ends, sending a signal to the project management process, organizational environment process and technical infrastructure process.

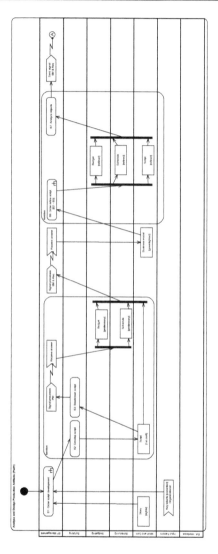

Figure 45: Activity diagram of the production process: Analysis and Design (1 of 2)[169]

---

[169] This table serves as overview, please see Appendix 8 to 10 (pp. 152-154) for an enlarged version

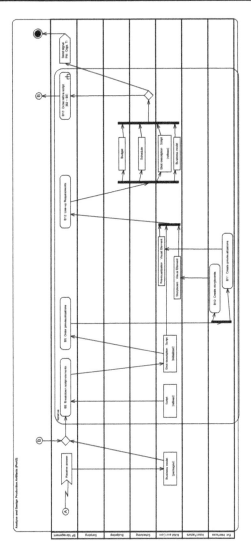

Figure 46: Activity diagram of the production process: Analysis and Design (2 of 2)[170]

The implementation and test process modeled in Figure 47 creates the actual media content. The goal of this process is to produce every single media element requested in the analysis and design process. The process is initialized when the production of media elements is scheduled. The action steps loop until no further media element is scheduled for production. The business process management server basically accesses the external interfaces and the media asset management and communications component. Furthermore necessary adjustments to the created media elements may impact the scripting, scheduling and budgeting components. During the implementation and test process, the business process management server supervises the requirements of each media element. These requirements are stored within the MPEG-7 meta-description of the element. Media files are imported through interfaces to external systems like digital cameras or specialized software solutions. The business process management server ensures that an imported file is indexed directly. The rights to the file are then managed before it is compressed, encrypted and stored within a database. In a similar way, the file is accessed via the media asset management and communications component. The business process management server controls the quality and attributes of the media file with respect to the requirements and decides whether adjustments have to be made or the media file can be finalized. The implementation and test process also follows the creative reference process.

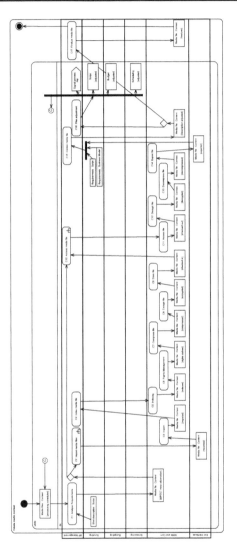

Figure 47: Activity diagram of the production process: Implementation and Test[171]

---

[171] This table serves as overview, please see Appendix 14 to 16 (pp. 158-160) for an enlarged version

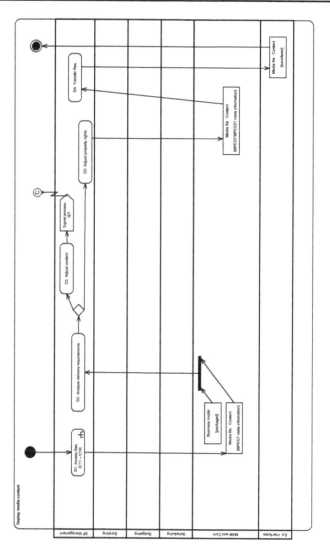

Figure 48: Activity diagram of the production process: Deployment[172]

---

[172] This table serves as overview, please see Appendix 17 to 18 (pp. 161-162) for an enlarged version

The deployment process is modeled in Figure 48. Its aim is to transfer the finalized media files and the mastered end product to the studio. The process is initiated when, during the post-production phase, the last media file is processed within the implementation and test process. The business process management server calls the media asset management and communications component to access the files and to export them via the external interfaces. The files are accessed as described in the implementation and test process. The files are then compared with the requirements set during the business modeling and requirements process. If the content matches the requirements, the property rights are adjusted and the files are delivered.

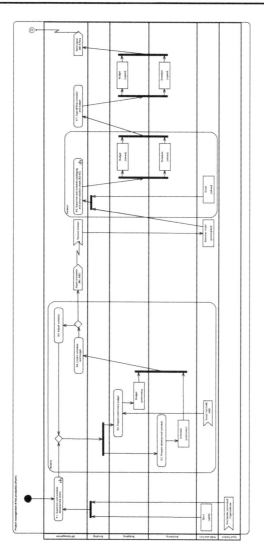

Figure 49: Activity diagram of the supporting process: Project Management (1 of 2)[173]

---

[173] This table serves as overview, please see Appendix 19 to 21 (pp. 163-165) for an enlarged version

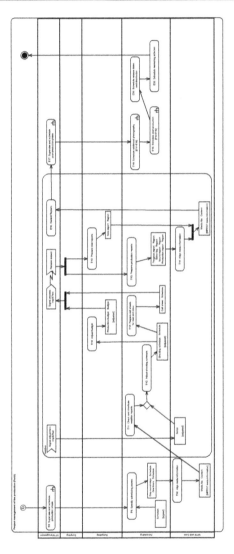

Figure 50: Activity diagram of the supporting process: Project Management (2 of 2)[174]

---

[174] This table serves as overview, please see Appendix 22 to 24 (pp. 166-168) for an enlarged version

The project management process is modeled within the two activity diagrams Figure 49 and Figure 50. The goal of the project management process is to supervise the schedule and budget throughout the production process. The business process management server must therefore address the scheduling and budgeting component, as well as the media asset management and communications component. The project management process can be divided into the development, the pre-production, the production and the post-production phase. In each phase, the process has to supervise and schedule the necessary activities – the scheduling action steps are iterative. As previously mentioned, the schedule and budget are dependent on each other, which is why they are accessed in parallel. The process is interrupted between phases, waiting for a signal from other processes to complete. During the production phase, the project management process is responsible for acquiring all the important production reports, which are then approved by the management. The information of these artifacts is used to describe the digital content elements using the MPEG-7 meta-description.

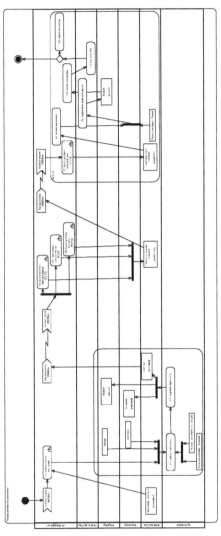

Figure 51: Activity diagram of the supporting process: Organizational Environment[175]

[175] This table serves as overview, please see Appendix 25 to 27 (pp. 169-171) for an enlarged version

The organizational environment process shown in Figure 51 handles the human resource management. The goal of the process is to form a production network and to handle the transactions. When the story rights are contracted within the business modeling and requirements process, an initializing signal is sent to the organizational environment process to select and hire key talents. Again, each "select and hire" action step is a complex action marked with a fork, following the reference process "select and hire" discussed above. The subsequent action steps for selecting and hiring personnel, investors and distributors are executed within the input factor market component. Further components accessed by the business process management server are the media asset management and communications component, as well as the scheduling, budgeting, and financial management components where artifacts such as contracts are stored. The process is interrupted at the end of each phase, waiting for a signal from the business modeling and requirements process to further expand the production network.

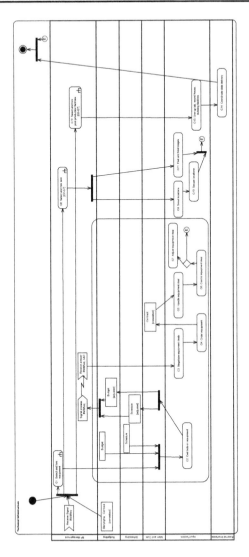

Figure 52: Activity diagram of the supporting process: Technical Infrastructure[176]

---

[176] This table serves as overview, please see Appendix 28 to 30 (pp. 172-174) for an enlarged version

The technical infrastructure process is modeled in Figure 52. Its goal is to facilitate the necessary technical infrastructure throughout the production process. For this the business process management server accesses the input factor market whereas artifacts from the media asset management and communications, scheduling, and budgeting components are read out and adjusted. Comparable to the organizational environment process, the basic action steps are "select and hire" steps following the reference process. The process is divided into the hiring of three different technical elements: equipment deals, sets and locations, and post-production facilities.

6 Conclusions

At the outset of my analysis I addressed the motion picture industry's value chain and the production process theoretically. I described strategic decisions made by movie production companies and discovered that the prevailing form of movie production organization is the project network, a specific form of the business web. I described the impact, an implementation of the MPEG-7 standard might have, in describing media content during the movie production process.

After that I elaborated on modern IT and IS strategy, concluding that the Service Oriented Architecture is the architecture model most appropriate for supporting the movie production process. I then described reference modeling in general and my chosen modeling process in particular.

I designed a framework to break the production process down into phases and processes. Here I chose the Rational Unified Process, a software development process model and modified it to meet the needs of the movie production process. I then modeled numerous use case diagrams with the Unified Modeling Language (UML2), describing the movie production process from the start of development to the end of post-production. The information taken from twelve expert interviews held at a major Hollywood movie production company in summer 2004 was modeled in the diagrams. Observations from my visits to a major Hollywood movie production company and my on-set collaboration with the short movie production "Entity: Nine" are included as well. Finally, I took part in the Movie Business Seminar of Prof. Jason E. Squire at the School of Cinema-Television in summer 2004, covering the entire product lifecycle of a motion picture.

The case study completes my analysis of the production process. I was able to identify the essential use cases of the various phases in a movie production and structure them into different processes. I described the responsible actors in the use cases, as well as most other involved actors, where reasonable.

I extracted those use cases that can be supported by information technology and examined existing systems. All use cases affected in any way by the digitization process were then identified. Descriptions of the activities, actors and created artifacts in each use case supply the information required for building the reference architecture models. I tried to optimize the process as much as possible and to integrate the existing, but well-established, software solutions into a single platform. I showed that the integration of management processes and digital data handling optimizes the digital movie production process. My developed reference model is based on models for organizational architecture, data architecture, application architecture, technical architecture and information architecture.

In this thesis, I addressed positive and normative research questions. I used desk research and case study research methods to gain theoretical insight into the movie production process as well as into IT and IS strategy issues.

I discovered that digitization permeates nearly every aspect of the movie production process. An IT and IS strategy calls for the integration of processes and data. In the analysis of the MPEG-7 description standard for digital content elements, I found that nearly every production step can be described, as can the syntax and the semantics of digital content elements. Therefore, the integration and management of digital elements on one platform seems to be an obvious and necessary milestone in harvesting benefits from a complete meta-description of content.

In analyzing the departments and actors of the production network, I specified their responsibilities and tasks in the various production phases, and assigned the tasks to either producing or supporting processes. The tasks were then classified in functional components.

My analysis disclosed that even Hollywood studios organize their movie production process in project networks. The IS and IT strategy must support the producer in his job as orchestrator of the network. Modern approaches to information systems architecture see the Service Oriented Architecture as the dominant model for at least the next decade. A Service Oriented Architecture enables the producer to control business processes via a management server, accessing specialized components necessary to fulfill the production process through web service interfaces. This architecture makes possible the flexible introduction of new components into the system without changing the underlying business logic. Specialized companies acting as independent partners within the production network can execute the individual component tasks.

A flexible production system not only addresses major Hollywood studios, which put together around 15 individually designed production networks a year. It also supports smaller production companies by reducing transaction costs incurred in managing the production process within the network.

Appendix

Legend:

- A accumulate
- M modify
- R read
- D delete
- X execute

Component / Phase codes:

- MPC — Input Factor Market Place and Contracts
- SCR — Scripting
- BLD — Budgeting
- SCH — Scheduling
- MAM — M&M and Communications
- FIN — Financing and Payment

- DEV — Development / Idea
- PAC — Packaging / Bundling, Distr. Finance
- PRE — Pre-production
- PRO — Production
- POS — Post-production

Processes	Phases	Use Cases	Components	Roles	Tech. Artifacts	Man. Artifacts
Business Modeling & Requirement	DEV	Acquire rights to story	MPC			Contract: A
		Develop script	SCR			
		Contract stars and talents	MPC			Contract: A
		Request team members	MPC			Contract: A
		Check crew availabilities	MPC			Contract: A
		Select and hire production supervisor	MPC			Contract: A
		Select and hire visual effects companies	MPC			Contract: A
		Secure all clearances and releases	FIN			
	PAC	Prepare a cash flow chart	BLD			
		Prepare recoupment plan	FIN			
		Find investors	MPC			
	PRE	Investigate product placement	FIN			
	DEV	Prepare preliminary budget	BLD			
Analysis & Design	BLD	Refine schedule and budget	SCR			
		Refine script	MPC			
	SCR	Get bids on equipment	MAM			
	PAC	Submit script to research company	SCR			
	SCR	Breakdown and refine script	SCR			
		Monitor changing script	SCR			
		Manage script new rites in time	SCR			
		Distribute scripts and paperwork	SCR			
		Breakdown n extras, stunts, effects etc.	MAM			
	MAM	Line-up requirements, green screen miniatures	MAM			
		Create previsualizations	MAM			
		Create storyboards	MPC			
Production Processes	PAC	Find and hold stages	MPC			
	PRE	Scout locations	MPC			
		Study past weather				
		Secure locations	PRE			

Appendix 1: Connection between use cases, roles and artifacts (1 of 4)

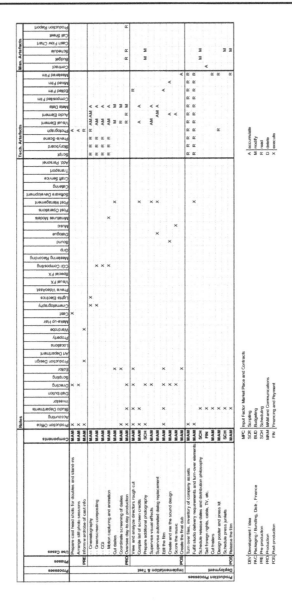

Appendix 2: Connection between use cases, roles and artifacts (2 of 4)

Appendix 3: Connection between use cases, roles and artifacts (3 of 4)

Processes	Phases	Use Cases	Components	Production Office	Accounting	Studio Departments	Investor	Distribution	Directing	Scripting	Editor	Production Design	Art Department	Locations	Property	Wardrobe	Make-up Hair	Cast	Cinematography	Lights Electrics	Previs Video-Asst.	Visual FX	Special FX	CGI Compositing	Mastering Recording	Grip	Sound	Dialogue	Music	Miniature Models	Post Operations	Post Management	Software Development	Catering	Craft Service	Transport	Add. Personel	Script	Storyboard	Previs-Scene	Photograph	Visual Element	Audio Element	Meta Data	Composited Film	Edited Film	Mixed Film	Mastered Film	Contract	Budget	Schedule	Cash Flow Chart	Call Sheet	Production Report
	DEV	Schedule and supervise the development activities	SCH																																																	A			
		Define pre-production schedule	SCH	X				X																																													A			
		Create final schedule	SCH	X				X																																													A			
		Sign-off on final budget	BUD	X	X			X																																										M					
	PRE	Create day-out-of-days	SCH					X																																												M			
		Check and distribute weather reports	SCH	X				X																																												M		A
		Adjust shooting schedules	SCH	X				X																																												M		
		Issue work calls	SCH					X																																												M		A
		Order stand-ins and extras	MPC					X									X																															A					A
		Prepare call sheets for cast and crew	SCH	X				X																																															A
		Monitor script changes	SCR	X				X																															MR													M	M			
		Prepare call sheets & production reports	SCH	X				X																																														A	A
		Submit daily/weekly production reports	SCH					X																																															A
		Prepare daily & weekly cost reports	BUD		X																																																		A
		Monitor schedule and budget	SCH	X	X	X																																													R	R			
	PRO	Control cash flow	BUD	X																																																M		
		Coordinate delivery of film to the lab	MAM	X																																	X			R					R								
		Oversee post-production activities	MAM																																		X			R	R		R	R	R	R					R			
	POS	Issue post-production schedule	SCH																																		X															A			

DEV	Development / Idea	MPC	Input Factor Market Place and Contracts	A	accumulate
PAC	Packaging / Bundling, Distr., Finance	SCR	Scripting	M	modify
PRE	Pre-production	BUD	Budgeting	R	read
PRO	Production	SCH	Scheduling	D	delete
POS	Post-production	MAM	MAM and Communications	X	execute
		FIN	Financing and Payment		

Roles

Tech. Artefacts

Man. Artefacts

Supporting Processes — Project Management

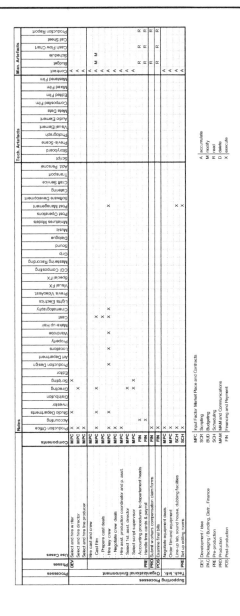

Appendix 4: Connection between use cases, roles and artifacts (4 of 4)

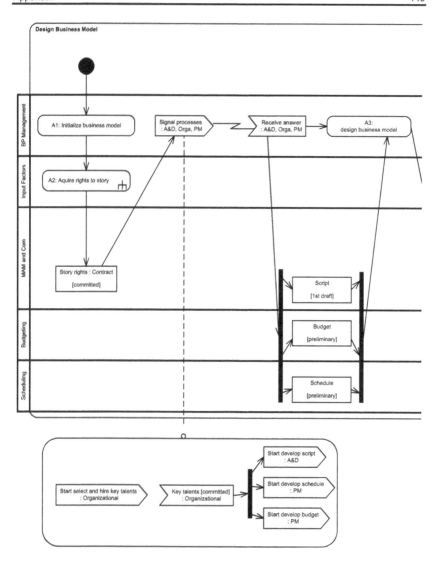

Appendix 5: Activity diagram of the production process:
Business Modeling and Requirements (1 of 3)

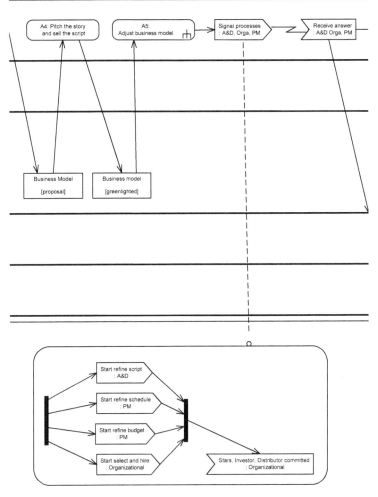

Appendix 6: Activity diagram of the production process:
Business Modeling and Requirements (2 of 3)

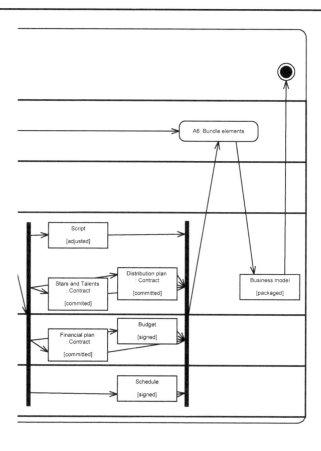

Appendix 7: Activity diagram of the production process:
Business Modeling and Requirements (3 of 3)

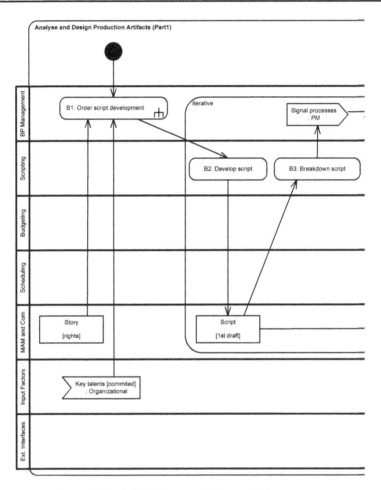

Appendix 8: Activity diagram of the production process:
Analysis and Design 1 (1 of 3)

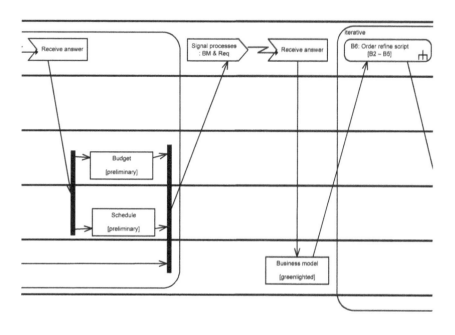

Appendix 9: Activity diagram of the production process:
Analysis and Design 1 (2 of 3)

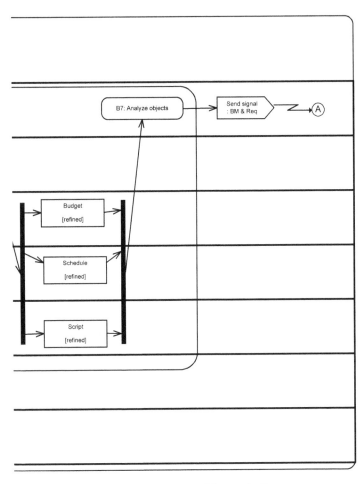

Appendix 10: Activity diagram of the production process:
Analysis and Design 1 (3 of 3)

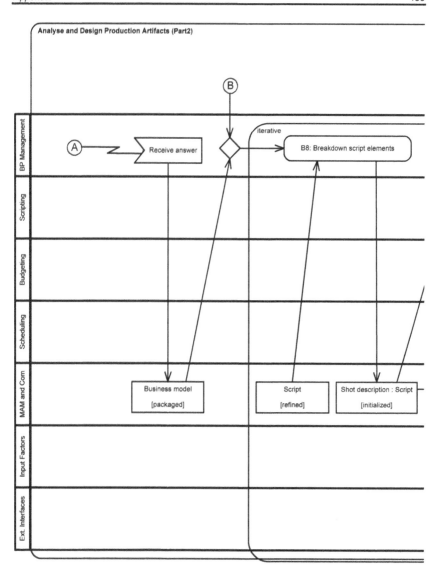

*Appendix 11: Activity diagram of the production process:
Analysis and Design 2 (1 of 3)*

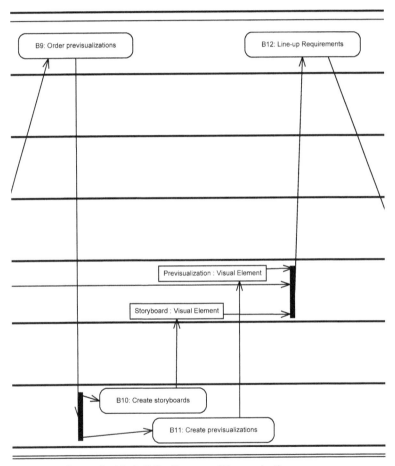

Appendix 12: Activity diagram of the production process:
Analysis and Design 2 (2 of 3)

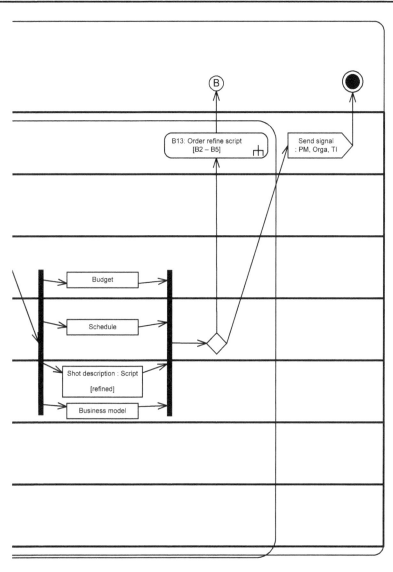

Appendix 13: Activity diagram of the production process:
Analysis and Design 2 (3 of 3)

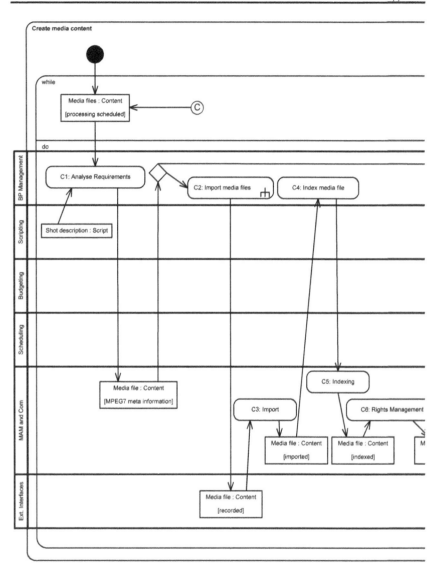

Appendix 14: Activity diagram of the production process:
Implementation and Test (1 of 3)

C10: Access media file

C7: Compress file

C9: Store file

C12: Decrypt file

ement

C8: Encrypt file

C11: Access file

Media file : Content	Media file : Content	Media file : Content	Media file : Content	Media file : Content	Media file : Co
[rights defined]	[compressed]	[encrypted]	[checked in]	[checked out]	[decrypted

Appendix 15: Activity diagram of the production process:
Implementation and Test (2 of 3)

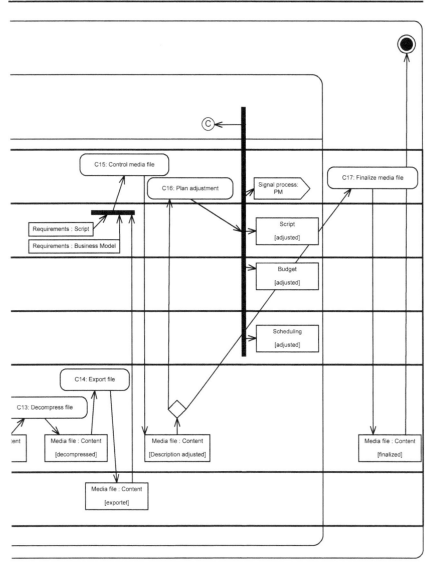

Appendix 16: Activity diagram of the production process:
Implementation and Test (3 of 3)

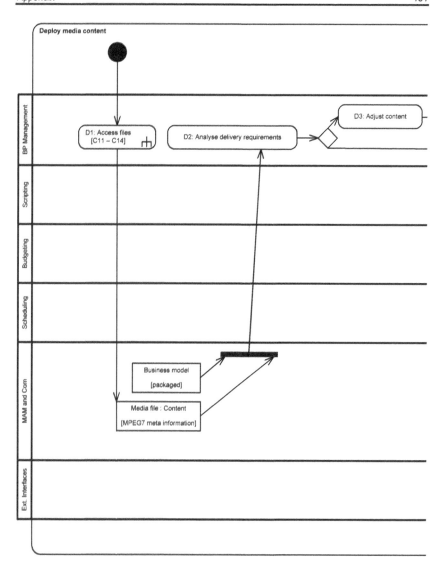

Appendix 17: Activity diagram of the production process: Deployment (1 of 2)

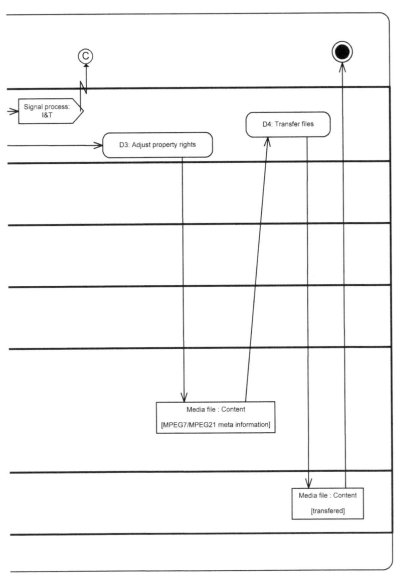

Appendix 18: Activity diagram of the production process: Deployment (2 of 2)

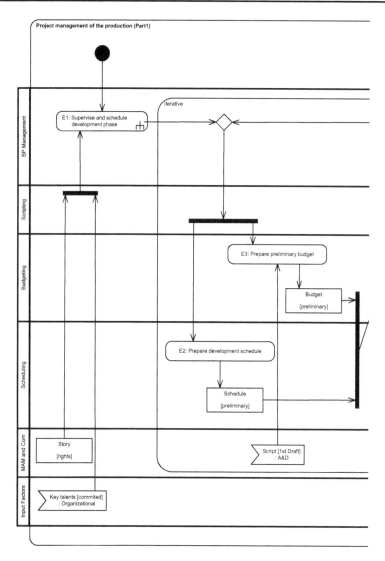

Appendix 19: Activity diagram of the supporting process:
Project Management 1 (1 of 3)

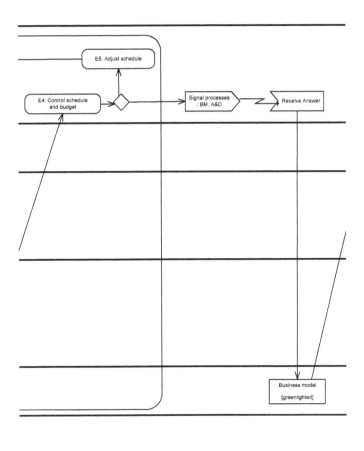

Appendix 20: Activity diagram of the supporting process:
Project Management 1 (2 of 3)

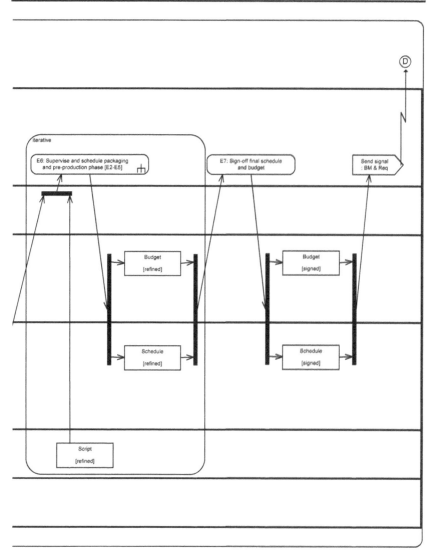

Appendix 21: Activity diagram of the supporting process:
Project Management 1 (3 of 3)

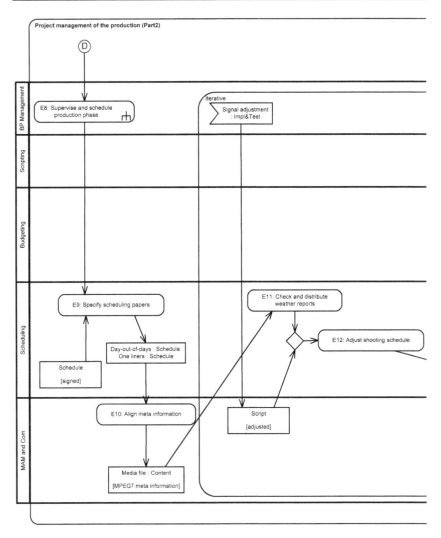

Appendix 22: Activity diagram of the supporting process:
Project Management 2 (1 of 3)

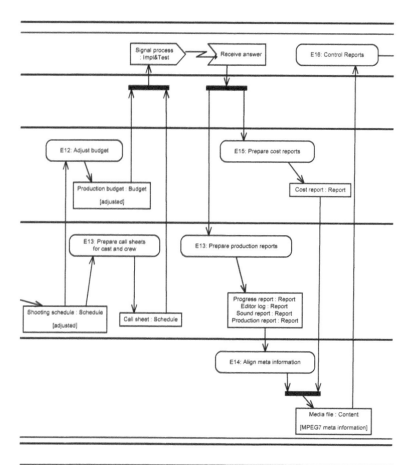

Appendix 23: Activity diagram of the supporting process:
Project Management 2 (2 of 3)

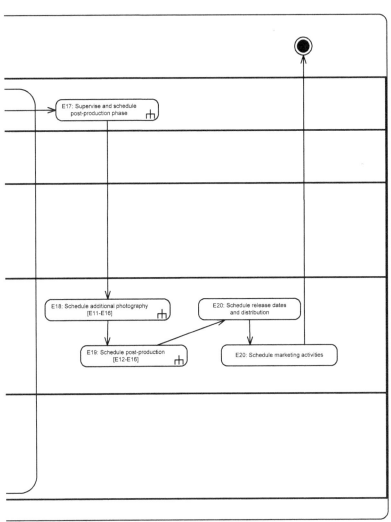

Appendix 24: Activity diagram of the supporting process:
Project Management 2 (3 of 3)

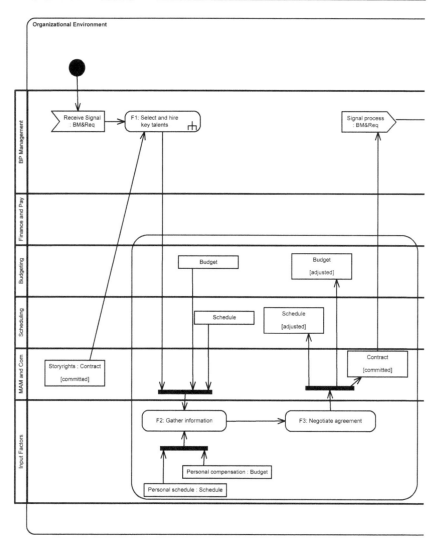

Appendix 25: Activity diagram of the supporting process:
Organizational Environment (1 of 3)

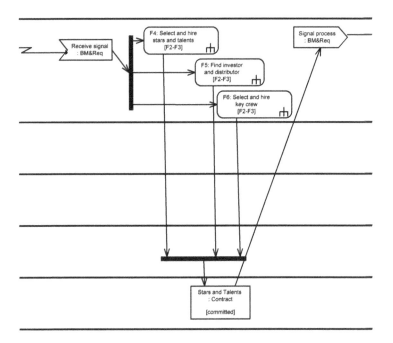

Appendix 26: Activity diagram of the supporting process:
Organizational Environment (2 of 3)

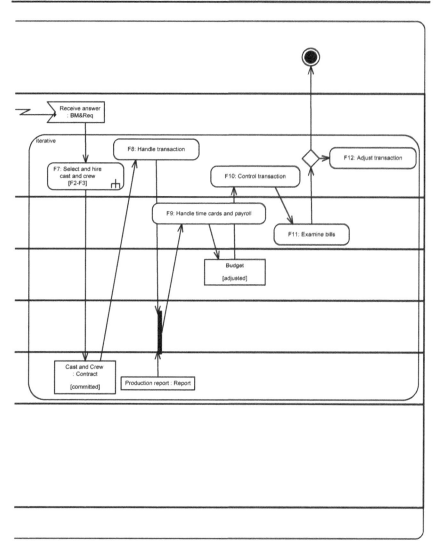

Appendix 27: Activity diagram of the supporting process:
Organizational Environment (3 of 3)

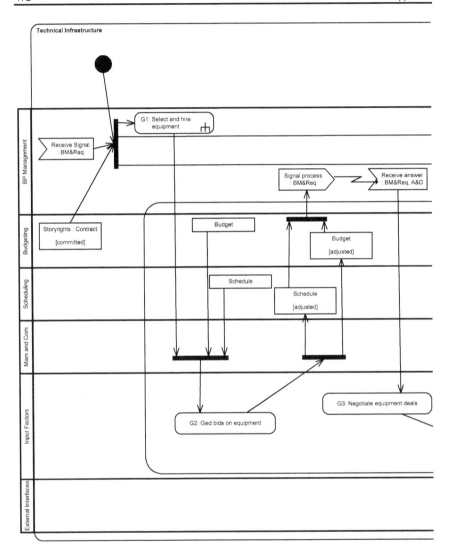

Appendix 28: Activity diagram of the supporting process:
Technical Infrastructure (1 of 3)

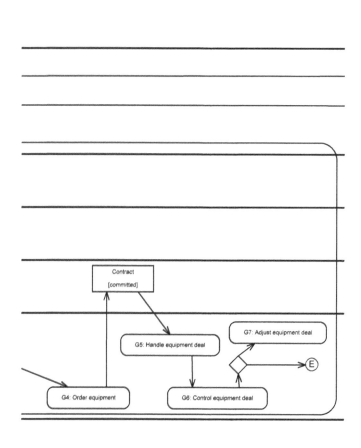

Appendix 29: Activity diagram of the supporting process:
Technical Infrastructure (2 of 3)

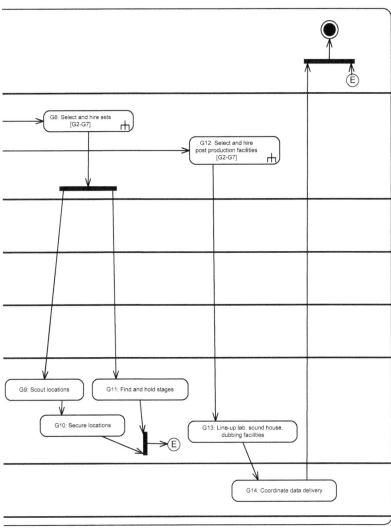

Appendix 30: Activity diagram of the supporting process:
Technical Infrastructure (3 of 3)

References

Abeck, S. (2005): Service Oriented Architecture [cited 04.05.2005]. Available from: www.cm-tm.uka.de/iswa.

Ainslie, A., Drèze, X., and Zufryden, F. (2002): Competition in the Movie Industry. UCLA / USC [cited 03.04.2003].

Albarran, A. B. (1997): Management of electronic media. Belmont: Wadsworth Publications.

Altmeppen, K.-D. (2003): Medien und Ökonomie. Vol. 1. Wiesbaden: Westdt. Verl.

Avid (2005): Avid Media Composer [cited 15.12.2005]. Available from: http://www.avid.com.

Backhaus, K. and Piltz, K. (1990): Strategische Allianzen. Zeitschrift für betriebswirtschaftliche Forschung 27.

Becker, J. (1995): Strukturanalogien in Informationsmodellen. Ihre Definition, ihr Nutzen und ihr Einfluß auf die Bildung von Grundsätzen ordnungsgemäßer Modellierung (GoM). In Wirtschaftsinformatik '95 - Wettbewerbsfähigkeit, Innovation, Wirtschaftlichkeit, edited by König, W. Heidelberg: Physica.

Becker, J. and Delfmann, P., eds. (2004): Referenzmodellierung. Heidelberg: Physica.

Becker, J. and Pfeiffer, D. (2006): Konzeptionelle Modellierung - ein wissenschaftstheoretischer Forschungsleitfaden. Paper read at Multikonferenz Wirtschaftsinformatik 2006, at Passau.

Biren, B., Dutta, S., and Wassenhove, L. V. (2001): Music on the Internet: Transformation of the Industry by Sony, Amazon.com, MP3.com and Napster. Insead [cited 26.11.2002]. Available from: http://elab.insead.edu/publications/cases/music_oninet.htm.

Bolstorff, P. (2001): How do I use SCOR? Supply Chain Council [cited 01.05.2006]. Available from: http://www.supply-chain.org/

Brocke, J. v. (2003): Referenzmodellierung - Gestaltung und Verteilung von Konstruktionsprozessen. Berlin: Logos.

Chan, J. O. (2005): Enterprise Information Systems Strategy and Planning. The Journal of American Academy of Business 2:148-153.

Chmielewicz, K. (1994): Forschungskonzeptionen der Wirtschaftswissenschaft. 3 ed. Stuttgart.

Dalet (2006): Dalet News Suite [cited 24.04.2006]. Available from: http://www.dalet.com/newsssuite.html.

Dearnley, J. and McKnight, C. (2001): The revolution starts next week: the findings of two studies considering electronic books. Information Services & Use 21 (2):65-78.

DeFillippi, R. J. and Arthur, M. B. (1998): Paradox in Project-Based Enterprise: The Case of Film Making. California Management Review 40 (2):125-139.

Dietl, H., Frank, E., and Opitz, C. (2005): Piraterie auf dem Tonträgermarkt und die Evolution von neuen Geschäftsmodellen in der Musikproduktion. Medienwirtschaft 2 (2):53-62.

Dietze, S. (2004): Modell und Optimierungsansatz für Open Source Softwareentwicklungsprozesse. Dissertation, Mathematisch-Naturwissen-schaftliche Fakultät, Universität Potsdam, Potsdam.

Digidesign (2005): Pro Tools HD [cited 15.12.2005]. Available from: http://www.digidesign.com/.

Digital Cinema Initiatives (2005): Digital Cinema System Specification [cited 13.04.2006]. Available from: http://www.dcimovies.com/DCI_Digital_Cinema_System_Spec_v1.pdf.

Eisenhard, K. (1989): Building Theories from Case Study Research. Academy of Management Review 14 (4):532-550.

Elberse, A. and Eliashberg, J. (2002): The Drivers of Motion Picture Performance: The Need to Consider Dynamics, Endogeneity and Simultaneity. Paper read at Motion Picture Industry Studies, at Florida Atlantic University.

Eliashberg, J., Swami, S., Weinberg, C. B., and Wierenga, B. (2003): Implementing and Evaluating SilverScreener - A Marketing Management Support System for Movie Exhibitors.

Entertainment Partners (2005): Movie Magic [cited 09.12.2005]. Available from: http://www.entertainmentpartners.com/.

Faulstich, W., ed. (2000): Grundwissen Medien. 4 ed, UTB für Wissenschaft. Große Reihe. München: Fink.

Ferstl, O. K. and Sinz, E. J. (2001): Grundlagen der Wirtschaftsinformatik. 4 ed. Vol. 1. München: Oldenbourg.

Frank, E. and Opitz, C. (2003): Julia Roberts, Tom Hanks & Co: Wie Stars zur effizienten Zuordnung von Filmen auf Filmkonsumenten beitragen. Wirtschaftswissenschaftliches Studium 32 (4): 203-208.

Gaitanides, M. (2001): Ökonomie des Spielfilms. München: Fischer.

Gaitanides, M., Scholz, R., and Vrohlings, A. (1994): Prozeßmanagement – Grundlagen und Zielsetzungen. In Prozeßmanagement – Konzepte, Umsetzungen und Erfahrungen des Reengineering, edited by Gaitanides, M., Scholz, R., Vrohlings, A., and Raster, M. München: Hanser.

Hammer, M. (1997): Das prozessorientierte Unternehmen - Die Arbeitswelt nach dem Reengineering. Frankfurt/Main: Campus.

Hammer, M. and Champy, J. (1994): Business Reengineering - Die Radikalkur für das Unternehmen. 4 ed. Frankfurt/Main: Campus.

Hansmann, H. (2003): Architekturen workflow-gestützter PPS-Systeme. Berlin: Logos.

Hass, B. H. (2002): Geschäftsmodelle von Medienunternehmen - Ökonomische Grundlagen und Veränderungen durch neue Informations- und Kommunikationstechnik. Wiesbaden: Gabler.

Heinrich, J. (1999): Medienökonomie Band 2: Hörfunk und Fernsehen. Opladen [u.a.]: Westdt. Verl.

Hess, T. (1996): Entwurf betrieblicher Prozesse: Grundlagen - Bestehende Methoden - Neue Ansätze. Wiesbaden: Gabler.

Hess, T. and Anding, M. (2002): Online Content Syndication - eine transaktionskostenorientierte Analyse. In Electronic Business, edited by Gabriel, R. and Hoppe, U. Heidelberg.

IBM (2006): Digital Media Framework [cited 24.04.2006]. Available from: http://www-03.ibm.com/solutions/digitalmedia/doc/content/resource/business/955416122.html?g_type=pspot.

IMDB (1993): Full cast and crew for Jurassic Park. Internet Movie Database [cited 09.12.2005]. Available from: http://www.imdb.com/title/tt0107290/fullcredits.

——— (1997): Full cast and crew for Titanic. Internet Movie Database [cited 09.12.2005]. Available from: http://www.imdb.com/title/tt0120338/fullcredits.

——— (2003): Full cast and crew for The Lord of the Rings: The Return of the King. Internet Movie Database [cited 09.12.2005]. Available from: http://www.imdb.com/title/tt0167260/fullcredits.

——— (2005a): Full cast and crew for King Kong. Internet Movie Database [cited 09.12.2005]. Available from: http://www.imdb.com/title/tt0360717/fullcredits.

——— (2005b): Full cast and crew for Star Wars III - Revenge of the Sith. Internet Movie Database [cited 09.12.2005]. Available from: http://www.imdb.com/title/tt0121766/fullcredits.

——— (2005c): Movie Terminology Glossary. Internet Movie Database [cited 09.12.2005]. Available from: http://www.imdb.com/Glossary.

——— (2006): Full cast and crew for Entity:Nine. Internet Movie Database [cited 30.05.2006]. Available from: http://www.imdb.com/title/tt0790655/.

Interviewee_1. (2004): Production Services, Interview 01.07.2004. Hollywood studio location, CA.

Interviewee_2 (2004): Creative Executive, Motion Picture Production, Interview 01.07.2004. Hollywood studio location, CA.

Interviewee_3 (2004): President of Physical Production, Interview 08.07.2004. Hollywood studio location, CA.

Interviewee_4 (2004): Senior Vice President Physical Production, Interview 08.07.2004. Hollywood studio location, CA.

Interviewee_5 (2004): Business Affairs, Interview 08.07.2004. Hollywood studio location, CA.

Interviewee_6 (2004): President of Marketing, Interview 15.07.2004. Hollywood studio location, CA.

Interviewee_7 (2004): Producer and Editor, Interview 15.07.2004. Hollywood studio location, CA.

Interviewee_8 (2004): Executive Vice President of General Sales, Interview 22.07.2004. Hollywood studio location, CA.

Interviewee_9 (2004): Executive Vice President of General Sales, Interview 22.07.2004. Hollywood studio location, CA.

Interviewee_10 (2004): President Worldwide Home Entertainment, Interview 22.07.2004. Hollywood studio location, CA.

Interviewee_11 (2004): Vice President Interactive, Interview 29.07.2004. Hollywood studio location, CA.

Interviewee_12 (2004): Global Marketing and Media Consultant, Interview 30.07.2004. University of Southern California, CA.

Jost, W. and Scheer, A.-W. (2002): Geschäftsprozessmanagement: Kernaufgabe einer jeden Unternehmensorganisation. In ARIS in der Praxis, edited by Scheer, A.-W. and Jost, W. Berlin: Springer.

Kagermann, H. and Österle, H. (2006): Geschäftsmodelle 2010 - Wie CEOs Unternehmen transformieren. Frankfurt: Frankfurter Allgemeine Buch.

Kean, B. (2004): Entity:Nine [cited 18.11.2004]. Available from: http://www.entitynine.com/.

Keen, M., Adinolfi, O., Hemmings, S., Humphreys, A., Kanthi, H., and Nottingham, A. (2005): Patterns: SOA with an Enterprise Service Bus in WebSphere Application Server V6. IBM [cited 05.12.2005]. Available from: www.ibm.com/redbooks.

Keil, K. and Iljine, D. (2000): Der Produzent. Vol. 1, Filmproduktion. München: TR-Verlagsunion.

Köhler, L., Anding, M., and Hess, T. (2003): Exploiting the power of product platforms for the media industry – a conceptual framework for digital goods and its customization for content syndicators. Paper read at Proceedings of the third IFIP Conference on e-commerce, e-business and e-government, at Sao Paulo.

Krcmar, H. (2003): Informationsmanagement. 3 ed. Berlin et al.: Springer.

Kugeler, M. (2000): Informationsmodellbasierte Organisationsgestaltung Modellierungskonventionen und Referenzvorgehensmodell zur prozess-orientierten Reorganisation. Berlin: Logos-Verl.

Lampel, J. and Shamsie, J. (2003): Capabilities in Motion: New Organizational Forms and the Reshaping of the Hollywood Movie Industry. Journal of Management Studies 40 (8):2189-2210.

Löwer, U. (2005): Interorganizational Standards - Managing Specifications for Web-Based Business Relationships, Institute for Information, Organization and Management, Ludwig-Maximilians-University, München.

Martinez, J. M. (2004): MPEG-7 Overview (version 10). International Organisation for Standardisation [cited 04.11.2005]. Available from: www.chiariglione.org.

McClintock, P. and Demspey, J. (2004): Together at last. Daily Variety [cited 12.05.2004]. Available from: www.variety.com.

Mertens, P., Bodendorf, F., König, W., Picot, A., Schumann, M., and Hess, T. (2004): Grundzüge der Wirtschaftsinformatik. 9 ed. Berlin: Springer.

Moe, W. W. and Fader, P. S. (2002): Using Advance Purchase Orders to Forecast New Product Sales. Marketing Science 21 (3):347-364.

Neelamegham, R. and Chintagunta, P. (1999): A Bayesian Model to Forecast New Product Performance in Domestic and International Markets. Marketing Science 18 (2).

Oestereich, B. (2005): Analyse und Design mit UML2 - Objektorientierte Softwareentwicklung. 7 ed. München, Wien: Oldenbourg.

Pagel, S. (2003): Integriertes Content Management in Fernsehunternehmen. Wiesbaden: Deutscher Universitätsverlag.

Pereira, F. and Koenen, R. (2001): MPEG-7: A Standard for Multimedia Content Description. International Journal of Image and Graphics 1 (3):527-546.

Picker, G. (2001): Kooperatives Verhalten in temporären Systemen. Berlin: Duncker & Humblot.

Picot, A., Dietl, H., and Frank, E. (2005): Organisation - Eine ökonomische Perspektive. 4 ed. Stuttgart: Schäffer-Poeschel.

Picot, A. and Fiedler, M. (2002): Institutionen und Wandel. Die Betriebswirtschaft 62 (3): 242-259.

Picot, A. and Hass, B. H. (2002): Digitale Organisation. In Medienkultur im digitalen Wandel: Prozesse, Potenziale, Perspektiven, edited by Spoun, S. and Wunderlich, W. Bern, Stuttgart, Wien: Paul Haupt.

Picot, A., Reichwald, R., and Wiegand, R. T. (2003): Die grenzenlose Unternehmung - Information, Organisation und Management. 5 ed. Wiesbaden: Gabler.

Porter, M. E. (2000): Wettbewerbsvorteile Spitzenleistungen erreichen und behaupten (Competitive advantage). 6 ed. Frankfurt [u.a.]: Campus-Verl.

——— (2001): Strategy and the Internet. Harvard Business Review 79 (3):63-78.

Prahalad, C. K. and Hamel, G. (1990): The Core Competence of the Corporation. Harvard Business Review 68 (3):79-91.

Press, L. (2000): From P-books to E-books. Communications of the ACM 43 (5):17-21.

Rawolle, J. and Hess, T. (2000): New Digital Media and Devices. The International Journal on Media Management 2 (2):89-99.

Reinstein, D. A. and Snyder, C. M. (2000): The Influence of Expert Reviews on Consumer Demand for Experience Goods: A Case Study of Movie Critics [cited 03.04.2003].

Remus, U. (2002): Prozessorientiertes Wissensmanagement. Dissertation, Wirtschaftswissenschaftliche Fakultät, Universität Regensburg, Regensburg.

Rüggeberg, D. (2006): Digitales Kino 2006 - Eine aktuelle Betrachtung: Filmförderungsanstalt (FFA).

Scheer, A.-W. (1997): Wirtschaftsinformatik. Referenzmodelle für industrielle Geschäftsprozesse. 7 ed. Berlin: Springer.

———, ed. (2002): Aris in der Praxis: Gestaltung, Implementierung und Optimierung von Geschäftsprozessen. Berlin: Springer.

Schlagheck, B. (1999): Objektorientierte Referenzmodelle für das Prozess- und Projektcontrolling. Wiesbaden: Gabler.

Schulze, B. (2005): Mehrfachnutzung von Medieninhalten - Entwicklung, Anwendung und Bewertung eines Managementkonzepts für die Medienindustrie. Lohmar: Eul.

Schumann, M. and Hess, T. (2002): Grundfragen der Medienwirtschaft: eine betriebswirtschaftliche Einführung. 2 ed. Berlin: Springer.

————, eds (1999): Medienunternehmen im digitalen Zeitalter - Neue Technologien - neue Märkte - neue Geschäftsansätze. Edited by Schumann, M. and Hess, T. Wiesbaden: Gabler.

Schütte, R. (1998): Grundsätze ordnungsmäßiger Referenzmodellierung - Konstruktion konfigurations- und anpassungsorientierter Modelle, Neue betriebswirtschaftliche Forschung 233. Wiesbaden: Gabler.

Schwegmann, A. (1999): Objektorientierte Referenzmodellierung theoretische Grundlagen und praktische Anwendung, Gabler-Edition Wissenschaft Informationsmanagement und Controlling. Wiesbaden: Dt. Univ.-Verl.

Shapiro, C. and Varian, H. R. (2000): Information rules - A strategic guide to the network economy. Boston, Mass.: Harvard Business School Press.

Sharda, R. and Delen, D. (2002): Forecasting Box-Office Receipts of Motion Pictures Using Neural Networks [cited 04.03.2003].

Simonoff, J. S. and Sparrow, I. R. (2000): Predicting movie grosses: Winners and losers, blockbusters and sleepers. Chance 13 (3):15-24.

Sjurts, I. (2002): Strategien in der Medienbranche Grundlagen und Fallbeispiele. 2 ed. Wiesbaden: Gabler.

Squire, J. E., ed. (2004): The Movie Business Book. 3 ed. New York: Fireside.

Stachowiak, H. (1973): Allgemeine Modelltheorie. Wien, New York: Springer.

Staden, I. v. and Hundsdörfer, B. (2003): Majors planen digital roll-out... - Auswirkungen der digitalen Zukunft auf die Kinobranche: Filmförderungsanstalt (FFA).

Stähler, P. (2001): Geschäftsmodelle in der digitalen Ökonomie - Merkmale, Strategien und Auswirkungen. Lohmar: Eul.

Steiner, F. (2005): Formation and early growth of business webs. Heidelberg: Physica.

Studio System Inc. (2005): The Studio System [cited 09.12.2005]. Available from: http://www.studiosystem.com/.

Supply Chain Council (2005a): SCOR Reference Guide Version 7.0 [cited 01.05.2006]. Available from http://www.supply-chain.org/

——— (2005b): Supply-Chain Operations Reference-model Overview [cited 01.05.2006]. Available from http://www.supply-chain.org/

Sydow, J. and Windeler, A. (2002): Project Networks and Changing Industry Practices - Collaborative Content Production in the German Television Industry. Organizational Studies 23.

Sydow, J., Windeler, A., and Wirth, C. (2003): Markteintritt als kollektiver Netzwerkeintritt - Internationalisierung der Fernsehproduktion in unreife Märkte. Die Betriebswirtschaft 62 (6):459-475.

Tzouvaras, A. (2003): Referenzmodellierung für Buchverlage - Prozess- und Klassenmodelle für den Leistungsprozess. Göttingen: Cuvillier Verlag.

Walter, B. v. and Hess, T. (2003): iTunes Music Store: Eine innovative Dienstleistung zur Durchsetzung von Property-Rights im Internet. Wirtschaftsinformatik 45 (5):541-546.

Whiteman, B. (2004): Viv U finds Babelsberg taker. Daily Variety [cited 13.07.2004]. Available from: www.variety.com.

Wiegand, R. T., Mertens, P., Bodendorf, F., König, W., Picot, A., and Schumann, M. (2003): Introduction to Business Information Systems. Berlin: Springer.

Windeler, A. and Sydow, J. (2001): Project Networks and Changing Industry Practices - Collaborative Content Production in the German Television Industry. Organization Studies 22 (6):1035-1060.

Wirtz, B. W. (1999): Convergence Process, Value Constellations and Integration Strategies in the Multimedia Business. the International Journal of Media Management 1 (1):14-22.

——— (2003): Medien- und Internetmanagement. 3 ed. Wiesbaden: Gabler.

Yin, R. K. (2003a): Applications of case study research. 2 ed. Thousand Oaks, London, New Delhi: Sage Publications.

——— (2003b): Case Study Research - Design and Methods. 3 ed. Thousand Oaks, London, New Delhi: Sage Publications.

Zerdick, A., Picot, A., Schrape, K., and others (2000): E-Conomics. Strategies for the Digital Marketplace. 1 ed. Berlin [et al.].

────── (2001): Die Internet-Ökonomie. Strategien für die digitale Zukunft. 3 ed. Berlin [et al.].

────── (2005): Emerging Media - Communication and the media economy of the future. Berlin: Springer.

Index

GPSR Compliance
The European Union's (EU) General Product Safety Regulation (GPSR) is a set
of rules that requires consumer products to be safe and our obligations to
ensure this.

If you have any concerns about our products, you can contact us on

ProductSafety@springernature.com

In case Publisher is established outside the EU, the EU authorized
representative is:

Springer Nature Customer Service Center GmbH
Europaplatz 3
69115 Heidelberg, Germany